WONDERFUL WAVERLEY

Edinburgh in the Glory Days

By
Paul Anderson

Haymarket shed was renowned for the pristine appearance of its Pacifics, but the Waverley pilots in fully-lined BR black livery were maintained to the same standard for many years. On an unknown date during the mid-1950s, J83 0-6-0T 68481, one of the west end pilots, propels empty stock through Princes Street Gardens towards the station, proudly bearing a disc stating that this is No.1 pilot. It is high summer and the abundant foliage is a perfect complement to the classical lines of the National Gallery of Scotland and the portal of Mound Tunnel. Photograph W. Hermiston, The Transport Treasury.

Copyright IRWELL PRESS Ltd.,
ISBN 1-903266-34-3

Cover photograph: Waverley in all its glory! The commanding clock tower of the North British Hotel rises against dark clouds as the sun breaks through in the south to highlight A3 60089 FELSTEAD leaving platform 9 with the 12.05pm to Carlisle on 24 March 1951. This Gresley Pacific, in the short-lived BR blue livery, emerged from Doncaster Works in August 1928 and was the first new A3, as opposed to those rebuilt from A1s. Many engines seen at Waverley carried unusual, sometimes intriguing names. 60089 celebrated the racehorse that won the 1928 Derby. Several of the superbly kept Pacifics allocated to Haymarket shed in the west end of Edinburgh had something to celebrate about themselves. Back in 1932, while allocated to Doncaster and carrying its first LNER number 2743, FELSTEAD was used in trials on the up Leeds 'Breakfast Train' between Grantham and Kings Cross, hauling 310 tons and reaching 90mph at Essendine. It moved to Haymarket in February 1951, the last of several exchanges between England and Edinburgh in 1950-51, and stayed there until November 1960. Photograph John Robertson, The Transport Treasury.

First published in the
United Kingdom in 2003
by Irwell Press Ltd.,
59A, High Street, Clophill,
Bedfordshire MK45 4BE
Printed by Newton Printing

CONTENTS

Introduction and Acknowledgements

This book celebrates a station, and no ordinary station at that. Edinburgh Waverley and its approaches provided a spectacular and immensely photogenic theatre for the cream of East Coast motive power and its less glamorous brethren. Historical information concerning the railway system has been kept to a minimum. That was covered by *An Illustrated History of Edinburgh's Railways* by W.A.C. Smith and Paul Anderson, published by Irwell Press in 1995, which also included detailed maps. Instead, *Wonderful Waverley* is a portrait in words and pictures of the Scottish capital's world famous station, its magnificent surroundings, the engines and trains which served it and the running sheds which were so crucial. Photographs range from the mid-1930s to the mid-1960s, with an emphasis on the first half of the 1950s. This thirty year period is just a cameo of a station which has been around for a century and a half, yet the locomotives portrayed represent a hundred years of railway history, from 'Pugs' built for Leith Docks in the early 1880s to the demise of the 'Deltics' on principal East Coast expresses in the early 1980s.

Unlike the author's previous books with Irwell Press, this one pays a lot of attention to the engines themselves, including their origin, work, achievements, names and, indeed, character. Much factual information has been gleaned from the Railway Correspondence and Travel Society's excellent *Locomotives of the LNER* series, a monumental 36 year project which is one of the best treatises ever on a particular aspect of Britain's railways. In this context, the author would like to thank Pip Bloor for painstaking work on locomotive history, shed allocations and other details. *Wonderful Waverley* would not have been possible without dedicated photographers, especially the late John Robertson who recorded the everyday scene in Edinburgh during the 1950s. His efforts are now a priceless reminder of an era which seems light years away from life at the beginning of the 21st century. Equally important is the tender loving care which Barry Hoper lavishes on those precious fragile negatives that bring the past to life. *The Transport Treasury* is an appropriate title if there ever was one. In order to provide a touch of light relief from purely railway matters, a few

poignant quotations and some historical details about the city have been included. Thanks to Edinburgh Library and the Tourist Information web site for these. A critical reading by two notable students of railway matters, Tony Wright and Irving Nicol, has been invaluable and is much appreciated.

Finally, with motive power such a prominent feature of the book, the names of certain gentlemen appear frequently in the text and captions. These were the Locomotive Superintendents and Chief Mechanical Engineers of the North British Railway and, from 1923, the London & North Eastern Railway, who were responsible for the succession of machines which captured the imagination of several generations of enthusiasts. Many readers will be acquainted with them, but here is the complete list just for the record: T. Wheatley (1862-1874), D. Drummond (1875-1882), M. Holmes (1882-1903), W.P. Reid (1903-1919), W. Chalmers (1919-1922), Sir Nigel Gresley (1923-1941), Edward Thompson (1941-1946), Arthur Peppercorn (1946-1947).

Waverley and its Surroundings

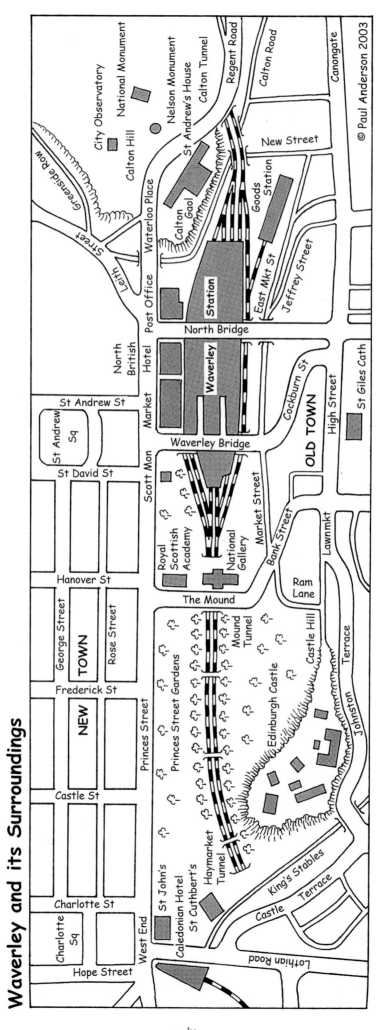

A Fine Prospect

'There was something grand about arriving at Waverley on a Midland or East Coast Scotch express. How joyously she shrilled as she skirted the distant misty bulk of the Salisbury Craigs! How proudly, even, she took the final plunge into Calton Hill tunnel! Thence you were brought, not to the ragged skirts of the city, as at Kings Cross or St Pancras, but to her very heart. In the evening haze, even Calton Gaol took on something of the savage grandeur of a Doré drawing, and this was by no means spoilt by the rising smokes of North British engines in the ravine below. Indeed the Gaol was mistaken for the Castle by innumerable tourists. In due course you rose out of Waverley's labyrinthine underworld, a place of stone, iron, smoky glass and crowds, filled by the harsh song of Westinghouse pumps, to find yourself in Edinburgh's midst. At once before you was the brilliant length of Princes Street, its rather vulgar Victorian condition gentled by the evening light, which likewise made the Scott Monument soar into a new and august dignity. Opposite, the Old Town glowed and smoked and sprawled up to the Castle Rock. Between the two, the North British Railway glimmered below the darkening gardens, plunged through the classically adorned Mound, its brilliant signal lamps and mounting smoke clouds flaunting the loveliness that nineteenth century romantics strove to deny.' From an article in *The Railway Magazine* by C. Hamilton Ellis, January 1941.

Just what was it that made Edinburgh, and Waverley itself, so wonderful? Mostly, it was a unique and complex amalgam of geology, geography and history. Geology is fundamental, the combination of volcanic and sedimentary rocks, together with the effects of the Ice Age, resulting in truly magnificent topography. Lava flows and the cores of long-extinct volcanoes gave rise to Arthur's Seat, Salisbury Crags, Castle Rock and Calton Hill. They are surrounded by less resilient sandstones, shales and, to the south east of Edinburgh, coal measures. In more recent geological history, sheets of ice pushed relentlessly from west to east, gouging out the valley now occupied by Princes Street Gardens, plucking away at the volcanic rocks to form the sheer crags below the castle and depositing the pile of debris on which Old Town now stands.

Geography dictated that an important settlement was bound to develop here. Edinburgh commanded the Firth of Forth, the most important sea approach to the Scottish lowlands, and nearby Queensferry was the easiest place to cross the estuary. With the Southern Uplands forming a barrier to the south, the obvious route to and from England was round the coast and Edinburgh commanded this as well. The Great North Road and East Coast railway both followed this course. Much of Edinburgh's long history has been one of conflict, reflected even today by the cluster of

Waverley as pure theatre. A group of onlookers, men and boys, husbands and wives, survey the grand panorama and unfolding drama from footpaths on The Mound. Some of them were probably there for the occasion. It is 28 July 1955 and A4 60009 UNION OF SOUTH AFRICA makes a determined start with the 4.00pm express to Glasgow Queen Street as A3 60097 HUMORIST lags behind a little with the 4.00pm to Perth. There was always a race between these two trains as far as Saughton Junction, where the Glasgow and Fife lines diverged. Although 60009 was in the lead here, the situation could change as a result of station work at Haymarket where both trains stopped. Given the 'right-away', the respective drivers would resume the race until their paths parted. Both Pacifics in this view were based at Haymarket shed, 60009 from new in June 1937 to May 1962 and 60097 from July 1950 to December 1961. Like so many A4s, UNION OF SOUTH AFRICA had some memorable moments. Originally 4488, it worked the last up 'Coronation' in 1939, one of the initial non-stop runs of the 'Flying Scotsman' when it was reintroduced in 1948, the first up service of the non-stop 'Elizabethan' in 1953 and the last up 'Elizabethan' in 1961. Photograph G.F. Heiron.

A little feather of steam in front of the chimney indicates that the glorious chime whistle of A4 60004 WILLIAM WHITELAW is echoing round the west end of Waverley. as the 5.15pm for Glasgow Queen Street gets underway from platform 14 during the summer of 1958. A rather larger cloud of steam drifts over the 1930s signal box, posing a temporary threat to concentration on the adjoining bowling green! The first three coaches are Gresley, Thompson and BR Standard vehicles respectively, each in carmine and cream livery, popularly known as 'blood and custard'. An A1 and two B1s are discernible elsewhere in the station. 60004, originally 4462, entered service in November 1937 and had spells at Kings Cross, Gateshead and Heaton before moving to Edinburgh in July 1941, the month its name was changed from GREAT SNIPE to that of the chairman of the LNER from 1923 to 1938. Photograph The Transport Treasury.

buildings forming the core of the Old Town huddled just below the castle. From the 1700s, it was a lot more peaceful and the city expanded by means of the New Town, in a fashion that could hardly have been more elegant. Associated with this development was that most curious of man-made creations, The Mound.

Most of the elements for the setting of Wonderful Waverley were in place by the time the Railway Age got underway, although to be honest, the station itself was not that wonderful for a half century or more. Edinburgh was important enough to be targeted by railway speculators at a fairly early date, the main line from Glasgow Queen Street to Haymarket opening in February 1842. Rails had been marching north from London towards Scotland since the late 1830s and a highly significant event was the completion of the North British route between Berwick and Edinburgh North Bridge during June 1846, followed by the extension of the Glasgow line through Princes Street Gardens to

North Bridge in August 1846. The station gradually adopted the name Waverley over the next few years. Before long, the trunk routes to Carlisle and Aberdeen were established and eventually an extensive inner and outer suburban network developed. At the end of the 19th century there were spectacular developments in the form of the Forth Bridge and the complete reconstruction of the station on a grand scale. Wonderful Waverley had arrived at last!

Going back to geology, geography and history, the route of the railway through Scotland's capital gave rise to some spectacular settings. There were almost aerial views from Calton Hill and The Mound, together with wonderful backdrops such as the foliage of Princes Street Gardens and the capricious architecture of Calton Gaol. In this theatre, engines magnificent and modest went about their daily business, many of them based in Edinburgh at St Margarets and Haymarket sheds.

Bottom right. In bright sunshine, the vast theatre of Edinburgh Waverley, as seen from The Mound, took on different guises according to the time of day. On the morning of 8 June 1961, with light coming from the south east, western aspects of the buildings and bridges dominating the station are in dark shadow and provide a heavy backdrop. Illuminated by the sun and undoubtedly the centre of attention, A4 60012 COMMONWEALTH OF AUSTRALIA leaves platform 16 with an Aberdeen express. The engine went new to Haymarket in June 1937 and stayed there until September 1963, less than a year before it was withdrawn. There is a Swindon Inter-City diesel multiple unit in platform 12 on a Glasgow Queen Street working. Photograph The Transport Treasury.

At the east end of Waverley there was a birds-eye view of the railway from Jacob's Ladder, a relentless flight of steps up Calton Hill from Calton Road. The year is 1960 and in low, early morning sunshine, A4 60027 MERLIN heads towards England with the up 'Talisman'. BR Mk 1 stock in maroon makes up most of the train. The signal cabin in the background was virtually a contemporary of the Pacific, which took up residence in Edinburgh as 4486 after completion at Doncaster Works in March 1937. In fact MERLIN spent all but the last three years and four months of its life at Haymarket. Photograph P Wilson, G R Whitelaw Collection.

The 22 North British Atlantics were impressive machines and C11 9877 LIDDESDALE in LNER green looks the part as it drifts through Princes Street Gardens with an express from the north one summer morning during the mid-1930s. In the distance is the Caledonian Hotel at Princes Street station, a most appropriate backdrop. During early Edwardian times, the North British decided that it needed something more powerful than traditional 4-4-0s to handle the heavier trains required to meet Caledonian competition. The 4-4-2 configuration, 6ft 9in driving wheels and a large boiler provided the necessary formula for hard work on steeply-graded and sharply-curved main lines, together with a fair turn of speed where possible. As 877, this particular engine was one of the first batch of fourteen built by the North British Loco Co at Hyde Park Works, Glasgow. It entered service at St Margarets in August 1906 for use on Aberdeen and Carlisle expresses. LIDDESDALE transferred to Haymarket with its designated crew during 1908 and later became notable for long spells of regular working to Newcastle, then Dundee. The Atlantics were squeezed out by Pacifics and Shires, so with boiler renewals imminent it was decided to scrap them. The end came for 9877 in April 1936. Photograph Dr Ian C. Allen, The Transport Treasury.

A Sense of Place

'Edinburgh pays cruelly for her high seat in one of the vilest climates under the heaven. The weather is raw and boisterous in winter, shifty and ungenial in summer and downright meteorological purgatory in the spring. The delicate die early, and I, as a survivor, among bleak winds and plumping rain, have been sometimes tempted to envy them their fate. For all who love shelter and the blessings of the sun, who hate dark weather and perpetual tilting against squalls, there could scarcely be found a more unhomely and harassing place of residence. Many such aspire angrily after the somewhere-else of the imagination, where all troubles are supposed to end. They lean over the great bridge which joins the New Town with the Old and watch the trains smoking out from under them and vanishing into the tunnel on a voyage to brighter skies. Happy the passengers who shake off the dust of Edinburgh, and have heard for the last time the cry of the east wind among her chimney tops! And yet the place establishes an interest in people's hearts; go where they will, they take a pride in their old home.'
From *Edinburgh, Picturesque Notes* by Robert Louis Stevenson, 1879.

When Roman legions under the leadership of Agricola marched north in AD79, they discovered that the Forth Valley was controlled by a Celtic tribe they called Votadinii, based at Dunedin, which was almost certainly the Castle Rock. The Romans never managed to subdue Caledonia and by AD211 had retreated behind Hadrian's Wall. Eventually, four warring kingdoms, the Picts, Scots, Britons and Angles occupied what is now Scotland. In the 9th century, Kenneth MacAlpin, King of Dalradia, managed to unite the territory by force and in 1035 his descendant, Duncan I, became the first King of Scotland. Half a century later, King Malcolm III established Edinburgh Castle and his wife Queen Margaret built a chapel within its walls, now the oldest building in the city. Her son, David I, built Holyrood Abbey a mile to the east and a small settlement grew up near the castle alongside the road to the abbey. Thus came into being the Old Town and Royal Mile.

Old Edinburgh was the scene of much strife, but many colourful episodes as well. When English forces captured the castle, Thomas Randolph,

nephew of Robert the Bruce, recaptured it by climbing its steep crags in the dead of night. Robert the Bruce granted Edinburgh a Royal Charter in 1329. St Giles Cathedral, a notable landmark with its open crown spire, took shape in the 14th and 15th centuries. From 1561 to 1572, the famous Protestant reformer John Knox was minister here and he delivered many thunderous sermons in the presence of Catholic Mary Queen of Scots, much to her discomfort. Besides historic buildings such as the Old Royal High School and Old Surgeon's Hall, there are the soaring tenements which proliferated in the 1600s, very early skyscrapers indeed. Even today, ancient street names reflect aspects of this illustrious past, whilst others are more enigmatic: Candlemaker Row, Cowgate, Canongate, Old Fishmarket Close, Grassmarket, Lawnmarket, Vennel and Pleasance.

For the last century and a half, the charisma and teeming activity of the Old Town has been mirrored down below at Waverley station. There was excitement with the first through trains to London, the opening of the Forth Bridge, the Railway Races to the

The almost hypnotic fascination of the steam engine is clearly apparent in this early 1930s view of the west end of Waverley, but pause for a while to take in the magnificent setting. On the left, Victorian facades of prestigious shops in Princes Street overlook that most glorious of open spaces, Princes Street Gardens. In turn, these are dominated by the elegant Edwardian bulk of the North British Hotel. Then come the monuments of Calton Hill and the turrets of Calton Gaol. On the right, a tram bound for the suburbs climbs North Bridge and buses head into town across Waverley Bridge. Even so, the scene would not be the same without Waverley West Cabin and the rather fine signal gantry. It is 3.30pm and V1 2916, which went new to Haymarket shed in July 1931, leaves the station with the 3.27pm to Larbert. The engine was withdrawn as 67616 in December 1962. An unidentified D11 Director backing on to the 4.00pm express for Glasgow Queen Street train can just be seen above the first coach. Photograph Dr Ian C. Allen, The Transport Treasury.

North and the inauguration of non-stop services to Kings Cross. For the interested observer, there was also a wonderful variety of locomotives. Take the 1930s, for example. Gresley A1 and A3 Pacifics were joined by streamlined A4s and the mighty P2 2-8-2s for the Aberdeen road. There were swansongs for the impressive C11 Atlantics of North British origin and Raven A2 Pacifics from the North Eastern. D29, D30, D31, D32, D33 and D34 4-4-0s mingled with interlopers in the form of D11 Directors and D49 Shires. Venerable G9 0-4-4Ts along with C15 and C16 4-4-2Ts shared the station with new V1 2-6-2Ts on local services. A quaint little D51 4-4-0T just made the beginning of the decade, but the Sentinel steam railcars named after long-vanished stagecoaches managed to chug through it. Capable J83 0-6-0Ts had a high profile on station pilot duties, while the diminutive Y9 0-4-0ST dock 'pugs' made occasional and sometimes celebrated appearances. These engines, and others not mentioned, had strange numbers to those enthusiasts brought up in the 1950s. It was, of course, reassuringly familiar during the first decade or so of BR, as depicted in the following pages. For the time being, let us celebrate those distant LNER days.

Although Pacifics eventually replaced the Atlantics on Edinburgh-Aberdeen expresses, loads increased to the extent that a single engine was often insufficient. Furthermore, double-heading by 4-6-2s would have put too much strain on certain structures, so smaller locos had to be used. Gresley's solution was the 2-8-2 wheel arrangement, a good example of his enthusiasm for designing individual classes to address specific problems. The four pairs of driving wheels gave greater adhesion and pulling power was considerably superior to a Pacific. P2 2001 COCK O' THE NORTH emerged from Doncaster Works in May 1934 and generated a lot of interest in view of its numerous innovations. The engine went on exhibition at Kings Cross and Waverley, was tested on a mammoth 586 ton train between Edinburgh and Aberdeen and spent over two months in France on trial. Normal duties from Haymarket shed commenced in June 1935 and until the war, 2001 regularly worked through to Aberdeen. Overlooked by The Mound and National Gallery in the distance and the fringe of the Old Town on the right, COCK O' THE NORTH sets off through Princes Street Gardens during the summer of 1936 with the 5.15pm to Aberdeen, which conveyed through coaches from the 'Flying Scotsman'. Along with its five sisters, 2001 was converted into an A2 Pacific in 1944. Photograph The Transport Treasury.

Below right. The western approach to Waverley was, and indeed still is, uniquely spectacular. Edinburgh Castle sits triumphantly on its massive pile of ice-ravaged volcanic rock, with the strange little Queen's Post Tower perched precariously above the gaunt crags. Opposite, a perfect foil is provided by the canopy of trees hiding the railway from the demure slopes of Princes Street Gardens. Closing the view is the Caledonian Hotel, its angular mass relieved by the spire of St Cuthberts and the tower of St Johns. Almost humbled by its surroundings, D29 9243 MEG MERRILIES, resplendent in LNER black with red lining, coasts towards Waverley with a stopping train from Fife in the early 1930s. Sixteen of these Reid 4-4-0s, provided with very large tenders, were built at Cowlairs Works in 1909-11 for non-stop Edinburgh-Carlisle workings. This was at a time when the North British and Midland were making a strenuous effort to compete with the Caledonian and LNWR for Anglo-Scottish traffic. The engines were given names derived from the novels of Sir Walter Scott, in this case the half-crazy gypsy woman from Kirk Yetholme in the Cheviots, featured in *Guy Mannering*. After many years of lesser duties, MEG MERRILIES was allocated BR number 62406, but was withdrawn in October 1949 before carrying it. However, the name was perpetuated on A1 60115, no stranger to Waverley. Photograph Dr Ian C. Allen, The Transport Treasury.

Another large signal bridge, this time under the control of Waverley East Cabin, was overlooked by the towers and ramparts of Calton Gaol. Waverley's impressive North British semaphores and signal boxes, dating from the reconstruction of the station at the turn of the century, had not long to go when this photograph was taken during the early 1930s. In 1936-38, colour lights operated by new concrete cabins were installed. Sporting 'Edinburgh' headboards and resting in the loco byes between jobs, are G9 9334 and V1 2924, both St Margarets engines, but quite a contrast. The former, designed by Reid and dating from September 1909, was one of the last 0-4-4Ts built for the North British. It may have come in from North Leith, but these tanks also worked the branches to Dalkeith, Glencorse, Penicuik and Polton. The latter, a Gresley loco completed in November 1931, was among the first 2-6-2Ts on the LNER and survived as 67624 until September 1960. It could have worked a North Berwick, Musselburgh, Leith Central or Suburban Circle train. Photograph Dr Ian C. Allen, The Transport Treasury.

Car 213 on route 11 from Fairmilehead to Stanley Road heads east along Princes Street during the bright sunny morning of 17 June 1956. There was a convenient stop opposite Waverley for any passengers from Braids, Morningside, Merchiston and Tollcross, or those heading home to Leith Walk, Pilrig and Bonnington. The southern terminus was cut back to Braids two months later, another victory for the buses. New Daimler/Alexander and Leyland/Metro-Cammell vehicles are following the tram. Although Edinburgh's medieval Old Town and Georgian New Town remained largely intact during the 19th century, Princes Street was rebuilt in a grand fashion by the Victorians. In this view, a further development was the 1930s Art Deco facade above the tram. Photograph John Robertson, The Transport Treasury.

Getting There

'Over and around all roared that Eighth Wonder of the World, Edinburgh's cable tramway system. The station has scarcely changed from then to now. True, where you once saw a somewhat ramshackle suburban train headed by an old Drummond engine, you now see a modern one hauled by a standard Gresley 2-6-2 V1 tank. The Eighth Wonder, too, has been replaced by something commonplace and electric. But the Waverley is still the best-placed station of any British city, and gives the arriving stranger a first impression rivalled in Europe only by the exclusively watery station approach at Venice.' From an article in *The Railway Magazine* by C. Hamilton Ellis, January 1941.

After Edinburgh's cable trams were belatedly replaced by electric traction, the system flourished and expanded. In its heyday there were 47 miles of route and a fleet of 360 cars. A decision to rely entirely on buses was made in 1952 and the last trams ran on 16 November 1956. When the network was at its maximum, it was possible to reach Waverley from most parts of the city by tram. These were the routes serving the station in 1938, at Princes Street, North Bridge and Post Office, as well as nearby Mound and George Street.

1 Liberton - North Bridge - Corstorphine
2 Granton - George Street - Stenhouse
3 Newington Station - Princes Street - Stenhouse
4 Piershill - Princes Street - Slateford
5 Morningside Station - North Bridge - Abbeyhill
6 West End - Post Office - Marchmont (Circular)
7 Liberton - North Bridge - Stanley Road
8 Granton Square - North Bridge - Newington Station
9 Granton Square - Princes Street - Colinton
10 Colinton - Princes Street
11 Fairmilehead - Princes Street - Stanley Road
13 Churchill - North Bridge - Granton (Circular)
14 Churchill - North Bridge - Granton (Circular)
15 Braids - Princes Street - King's Road
16 Braids - Princes Street - Granton Square
17 Newington Station - North Bridge - Granton Square
18 Liberton Dams - Waverley
19 Craigentinny Avenue - North Bridge - Tollcross
20 Joppa - Portobello - Post Office
21 Levenhall - Musselburgh - Post Office
23 Granton Road Station - Mound - Morningside
24 Comely Bank - Stockbridge - Waverley
25 Corstorphine - Princes Street - Craigentinny Avenue
27 Granton Road Station - Mound - Firrhill

Route 23 ran from Morningside station on the South Suburban line to Granton Road station on the Leith North branch, via The Mound. Passengers for Waverley had a short walk along Market Street and Waverley Bridge as this service barely touched Princes Street before heading along Hanover Street into the New Town. In May 1956, car 83 climbs up The Mound towards the Old Town, with the Church of Scotland Assembly Hall dominating the scene. Edinburgh's trams were painted deep red and white with gold lining and were invariably kept in superb condition. Such pride was even reflected by the owner's name on the lower panels, not Edinburgh Corporation, but 'City and Royal Burgh of Edinburgh'. This route, along with Braids - Stanley Road, were the only survivors on the last day. Photograph John Robertson, The Transport Treasury.

It was customary to keep the clock at the top of the North British Hotel tower a couple of minutes fast, so A2/1 60507 HIGHLAND CHIEFTAIN is leaving right on time with the 10.30am from Edinburgh Waverley to Newcastle Central, despite 10.32 on the dials. It was a crisp winter morning on an unidentified date in the early 1950s and very clear air combined with bright sunshine reveals the Baroque splendour of the hotel and the classical dignity of the Post Office in some detail. The gap between them, visible above the third coach, marks the approach to North Bridge. HIGHLAND CHIEFTAIN was one of the Thompson Pacifics built instead of the last four V2s, taking running numbers of the intended 2-6-2s, in this case 3696. As 60507, the loco was at Haymarket from December 1949 to July 1960. Clearly it is in very good condition, as there are none of the steam leaks which seemed to plague this particular batch of engines. The tender is from A4 4469 SIR RALPH WEDGWOOD which was bombed in York shed on 29 April 1942. Photograph John Robertson, The Transport Treasury.

The clock indicates just after 11.12am, so it is a punctual departure for 60031 GOLDEN PLOVER with the 11.10am Sunday service from Waverley to Kings Cross on 11 July 1954. A clear blue sky complements the sparkling green engine, red and cream coaches and just a touch of white exhaust, indicating maintenance, firing and driving to perfection. The A4 went to Haymarket as 4497 after completion at Doncaster Works in October 1937 and stayed there until February 1962. GOLDEN PLOVER was one of the A4s named after birds with a fast or powerful flight, in this case a 'strikingly handsome wader producing one of the most beautiful plaintive calls of any British bird', according to one description. They breed on upland moors, including those in Scotland, and are found in southern Britain in winter. Less frequent migrations than an A4, but how appropriate! Photograph John Robertson, The Transport Treasury.

Staying There

'Within the course of a few weeks the magnificent hotel of the North British Railway Company, which for the last five years has been slowly rising above the Waverley Station in Edinburgh, will be opened. To be accurate, the vast building will be ready for occupation in October. The fact is of considerable interest to the travelling public, many of whom, no doubt, have seen at different stages the rise of the palatial pile, and thought admiringly of the noble proportions of the building. It is, indeed, an important addition to Edinburgh's many architectural features. The site it occupies is one of the most conspicuous in the glorious city of the North.' From an article in *The Railway Magazine* by R. B. Mathieson, 1902.

A massive building in such a prominent place was bound to have an impact on the Edinburgh skyline and fortunately the North British was up to the task. For many years it was not a good railway, but the company's fortunes had been transformed by the Forth Bridge and much better management. No expense was spared on the hotel. Its most spectacular feature was the beautifully-proportioned 183ft clock tower, although the elegant roofline was just as important in the overall composition. When seen from different angles, the hotel had Calton Hill, Castle Rock, Arthur's Seat or Princes Street in the background and in each case the grand edifice actually enhanced the view.

Access to the main entrance hall and reception facilities was from Princes Street. This level also had a sumptuous suite of public rooms, notably the Palm Lounge, Coffee Room, Late Supper Room and Drawing and Reading Room. Decoration was elaborate, featuring mahogany panelling, wall hangings in silk, beautiful plaster friezes and Renaissance ceilings. Electric lighting was installed throughout and guests could make use of 'electric elevators' to reach the upper floors. Extensive kitchens, an ample wine cellar, cold storage for provisions and a laundry were provided. There was accommodation for 400, including special bachelor suites on the third floor. These included a sitting room, two bedrooms and a bathroom and were let by the year for 'gentlemen desiring to reside in the city'. No doubt rooms on the west side were especially popular, for they looked out on Princes Street Gardens, the Scott Monument, The Mound and Edinburgh Castle - one of the most famous views in the world.

Even a thick veneer of grime does not detract from the impressive profile of V2 60846 basking in the sun at the west end of Waverley one afternoon during the summer of either 1964 or 1965. The hotel clock shows 4.45pm and the train is probably bound for Perth. At the time, these workings were often entrusted to V2s based at St Margarets because of the unreliability of diesels. This particular 2-6-2 was completed at Darlington Works in February 1939 as 4817 and became something of a wanderer during its BR career. The engine was at Doncaster shed in 1950, Ardsley in 1955, Heaton in 1959, Thornaby in 1961 and finally migrated to Edinburgh during 1963. Photograph The Transport Treasury.

Although the best materials were employed and attention to detail was meticulous, the undoubtedly magnificent grand hall at Waverley was rather overpowering and a touch pompous. It was a classic example of unabashed opulence dating from the time when Victorian enterprise was evolving into Edwardian extravagance. This view, looking towards the north wall and its passageway leading to the up main platform, was taken in the early 1950s, but certainly no earlier than 1953 as there is a sign for the 'Starlight Specials' to London which began that year. In the foreground is the booking office for trains to the south and east, principally those via the East Coast and Waverley routes. Its dark woodwork incorporated sombre Baroque trappings, admittedly similar to contemporary facilities elsewhere. The mosaic floor had a floral pattern bordering the walls and in each corner a circular feature with 'The North British Railway Company' surrounding the appropriate coat-of-arms. Fortunately, plenty of daylight came through the highly decorative ceiling glass, including that in the central dome which had a frieze featuring Greek gods and goddesses supporting garlands. It is around 10.15am and numerous typists are at work in the first floor offices, but it seems the hall itself has been cleared of people for the photograph to be taken.

The Great Hall

'Occupying a central position at the west end of the central block is the booking hall, notable for its fine mosaic floor, ornamental stone and wrought-iron work, its lofty glazed roof, in the centre of which is a dome, also glazed, which with the large windows in the west wall effectively light up the interior. The booking office is placed near the centre of this spacious hall and is octagonal in shape, its east and west sides being longer than the others, the massive oak cabinet work of which it is constructed being one of its distinctive features. It has 13 booking windows allocated for traffic on the various routes going south and east, and, on the whole, a very pleasing and artistic effect has been obtained. Access is gained to the booking hall from the west by two entrances: from the up platform and down platform sides by passage-ways, paved in mosaic like the booking hall, and from the east by two long passages, paved in oak parquetry.' From an article in *The Railway Magazine* by J. F. Gairns, 1926.

When these observations were made, the LNER was very much in its infancy and little had changed since North British days or, for that matter, since the station had been built. There were two clocks in the booking hall, one on the north side supported by an ornamental wrought iron bracket and another on the west wall described as 'a synchronised clock which registers Greenwich mean time'. Also on the west side was a life size bronze statue of the late John Walker, former General Manager of the North British Railway. Alongside were models of the ROCKET and NB Atlantic 872 AULD REEKIE. In the centre of the east side was a large bronze war memorial with the names of North British employees who gave their lives in the 1914-18 conflict. On the north side of the booking hall was the ladies first-class waiting room and in the north passage a general waiting room, as well as an entrance to upper floor offices. The south side, together with its passageway to the platform, had seat reservation, sleeping berth and season ticket offices, along with another stairway to the first floor offices.

Outside, facing the up main platform, were the LMS enquiry office, left luggage office, shop parcels and cloakroom counter, telegraph office, third class refreshment room and hoists linked to the Post Office by an overhead gangway. On the down side were waiting rooms, the stationmaster's office and lost property office. Facing the eastern bay platforms were a first class refreshment room and a large tea and dining room. Between them, passages around one of the piers of North Bridge led to lavatories and the booking hall. Also facing the bays was a model of a North British 4-4-0 with a collecting box for the Railway Servants Orphanage. Beyond the cab road at the west end were two octagonal buildings, one incorporating a bookstall and the other a second booking office.

The north and west booking office was on the western concourse, between the taxi rank and the buffer stops of platforms 14 and 15. In this early 1950s scene, the nearest windows are headed 'Glasgow and the West, Corstorphine, Dalmeny, Larbert, Ayr, Ireland' and 'Fife and the North via Forth Bridge' respectively. The Waverley Buffet occupies the rear section of the booking office building and a John Menzies bookstall is part of a matching structure on the right. In the background, one of the vehicle ramps incorporating a pavement for pedestrians rises towards Waverley Bridge.

The vast roof over the east end platforms extended almost to the ramps and was finished off with a fine screen, the base of which described two graceful parabolic curves. Outside the train shed, immediately to the south, stood the island platform of the suburban station. On Saturday 29 August 1953 it played host to the 10.30am express for Kings Cross, seen leaving behind A3 60037 HYPERION. This engine, named after the winner of the 1933 Derby and St Leger, went new to Haymarket in July 1934 and was based in Edinburgh until withdrawn from St Margarets during December 1963. In March 1938, still numbered 2502, it became the first Pacific to be allocated to St Margarets specifically for working the mid-day express to Carlisle. HYPERION returned to Haymarket exactly a year later. Photograph John Robertson, The Transport Treasury.

Acres of Glass

'Design and finish are of the most approved type, and no device has been neglected which could promote the comfort and convenience of passengers. The total area occupied is 23 acres, 11½ of which are under glass. Of the remainder, 5 acres are set apart for the goods station. There are three sections, namely (1) the chief passenger station, (2) the suburban passenger station and (3) the goods station. The principal station consists of two main platforms each extending over its entire length of 560 yards, together with 15 dock platforms, in length from 180 yards upwards - Nos. 1 to 8 being at the East end and Nos. 9 to 15 at the West end. Northernmost main platform is the "main up" and southernmost "main down". Including those set aside for suburban traffic - also stretching the whole length of the station - the aggregate length of the platforms is 4,660 yards or about 2¾ miles, and 358 carriages can be accommodated alongside at one time. There are 8 main lines and 56 roads and sidings, worked by 290 signals and 228 points from 5 signal cabins, the East end cabin having the largest locking frame all in one piece in the world. The main part of the station is an "island" with a width of 285 feet between the up and down main lines.' From an article in The Railway Magazine by John Robertson, 1912.

Despite its size and opulence, Waverley suffered from two disadvantages. One was basically cosmetic, but the other was more serious as far as passengers were concerned. Firstly, the city fathers required the North British to restrict the vertical height of the station to 42ft above rail level. Consequently, there was no soaring roof like the one constructed at Leith Central a few years later. Instead, a succession of shallow glazed gables rose from transverse lattice girders supported by a forest of columns with decorative capitals and bases. The stone screen walls at either side also had plenty of ornamental work. Overall, the effect was very pleasing, although the station could never be described as one of the great cathedrals of the steam age. The second drawback was access. There was no grand entrance building and, in fact, the busiest pedestrian approach was the Waverley Steps, that notorious stone stairway down from Princes Street. This led to the main footbridge, which also served the suburban island platform and also continued to Market Street on the south side of the station, thus providing another way in. From Waverley Bridge two ramps led down to the concourse, one for arriving cabs and the other for those departing, although there were pavements for pedestrians.

Whatever the drawbacks, there was more than ample compensation when it came to the trains. In early LNER days, Waverley dealt with about a thousand trains a day. They included inner suburban services, outer suburban workings, stopping trains on rural routes, fast services to other Scottish cities, expresses to England and long distance cross-country workings, including through coaches from as far away as Penzance. Dealing with traffic at Waverley was a lot more complicated than at a conventional city terminus because of the amount of detachment and attachment of coaches and fish vans, as well as the transfers between bay and through lines. At times, four pilot engines were busy simultaneously. Even then, train engines had to do their share of the remarshalling. Matters were made slightly easier by extending some workings beyond Edinburgh. For example, certain Glasgow trains continued to Leith Central or North Berwick. Satisfying the needs of restaurant cars and sleeping cars also had to be borne in mind. Even between 3.30am and 4.30am there was a hive of activity as two trains arrived from Kings Cross, engines were changed, and sleeping cars and through coaches to Perth, Inverness, Aberdeen, Lossiemouth, Glasgow and Fort William were reformed into three trains.

A couple of East Coast Pacifics had names that young enthusiasts found almost impossible to pronounce. One of these was A2 60530 SAYAJIRAO, dedicated to the winner of the 1947 St Leger, a racehorse owned by the Maharaja of Baroda. This explains the unfamiliar name, which belonged to a Gujurati Maharaja, or king, way back in Indian history. On an unknown date in the early 1950s, SAYAJIRAO is neatly framed by the east end of the station roof as it leaves Waverley with the up 'Queen of Scots' Pullman, which it will take as far as Newcastle. The engine emerged from Doncaster Works in LNER green and went to Kings Cross shed as E530 during March 1948. BR green was applied in December 1949, immediately before 60530 was transferred to Haymarket where it stayed until October 1961. Photograph John Robertson, The Transport Treasury.

Eight bay platforms were provided at the east end of Waverley, mainly for local services. In this 1935 scene, shafts of sunlight cut through the smoke haze as D34 9504 GLEN ALADALE and a steam railcar wait to leave for Hawick and North Leith respectively. The Glen was always a St Margarets engine and was withdrawn from that shed as 62488 in October 1960. Several Sentinel railcars, all named after long-forgotten stagecoaches, were allocated to St Margarets in the 1930s. This one was no doubt one of ROYAL EAGLE, QUICKSILVER, PEARL or NETTLE, which were in Edinburgh at the time. Photograph H.N. Shepherd, The Transport Treasury.

At the west end of Waverley the overall roof only extended as far as Waverley Bridge, umbrella canopies sheltering the outer reaches of the platforms. In this April 1957 scene, the bridge can be seen five coaches down the train, almost closing the view. Haymarket A4 60027 MERLIN has arrived with a service from Perth, Dundee or Aberdeen and already carries a single lamp for its light engine movement back to the shed. In late LNER and early BR days, MERLIN became something of a chameleon, displaying five different liveries in 5½ years. From the beginning of 1947 to mid-1952 it was, respectively, wartime black, LNER blue, BR purple, BR blue and finally the familiar Brunswick green. Photograph D.H. Beecroft, The Transport Treasury.

The Governor's House

'Return thither on some clear, dark, moonless night, with a ring of frost in the air, and only a star or two set sparsely in the vault of heaven and you will find a sight as stimulating as the hoariest summit of the Alps. The solitude seems perfect; the patient astronomer, flat on his back under the observatory dome and spying heaven's secrets, is your only neighbour; and yet all round you there comes up the dull hum of the city, the tramp of countless people marching out of time, the rattle of carriages and the continuous keen jingle of the tramway bells. An hour or so before, the gas was turned on; lamp-lighters scoured the city; in every house from kitchen to attic, the windows kindled and gleamed forth into the dusk. And so now, although the town lies blue and darkling on her hills, innumerable spots of the bright element shine far and near along the pavements and upon the high façades. Moving lights of the railway pass and re-pass below the stationary lights upon the bridge. Lights burn in the jail. Lights burn high up in the tall lands and on the Castle turrets, they burn low down in Greenside or along the Park. They run out beyond the other into the dark country. They walk in a procession down to Leith and shine singly far along Leith Pier.' From Edinburgh, Picturesque Notes by Robert Louis Stevenson, 1879.

There are wonderful views from Calton Hill day or night, but there is much more to this rugged little outcrop of volcanic rock in the middle of Edinburgh. For many years it was a favourite site for erecting monuments and miscellaneous buildings. Although Robert Louis Stevenson mentions an observatory, there are actually two of them on the summit, the Old Observatory designed by New Town architect James Craig in 1792 and the City Observatory built in 1818. Battles provided an excellent excuse for building activity. For example, the naval victory at Trafalgar in 1805 gave rise to Nelson's Tower. The most prominent of all is the unfinished acropolis, grandly initiated as the 'National Monument' in 1816, a year after the defeat of Napoleon at Waterloo. It was meant to be a replica of the Parthenon in Athens and a tribute to those who had died in the Napoleonic Wars. Construction work began in 1822 to the design of accomplished Edinburgh architect William Playfair, but funds were soon used up and only the façade was completed. Condemned as 'Edinburgh's Shame' at the time, the unfinished edifice soon became regarded with much affection.

These eccentric artefacts on the summit of the hill overlooked a much more dour place above the sheer southern crag. Calton Gaol resembled a medieval fortress. Indeed, as mentioned in an earlier quote, many visitors thought it was the castle. Two centuries ago, even something as serious and sombre as a prison demanded special architectural treatment, one such manifestation being the rotund, whimsical tower house where the governor resided. Since 1846 it has overlooked the railway, providing a backdrop worthy of Walt Disney for passing trains. Following the demise of Calton Gaol, St Andrews House was built on part of the site. Although it had a prosaic function housing the Scottish Office, the 1937 Art Deco building was unusual and interesting enough to enhance Waverley's eastern approach.

The Governor's House keeps watch over V1 67659 as it leaves Waverley with a North Berwick train on 10 April 1952. This engine was one of a batch of V1s that went new from Doncaster Works to Tyneside in 1935-36. As 465, it entered service at Blaydon shed during May 1936 and worked local trains to places such as Blackhill and Haltwhistle. After spending 1939 at Middlesborough for the hourly Newcastle services, it was transferred to St Margarets and remained there until withdrawn in February 1962. Out of the class of 92 locos, it was one of only 18 which were not converted to, or built as, the more powerful V3s with higher boiler pressure. Photograph John Robertson, The Transport Treasury.

Above. A good impression of the sheer crag of volcanic rock below Calton Gaol can be gleaned from this view of the east end of Waverley on 29 August 1953. Thompson A2/3 60521 WATLING STREET of Gateshead shed departs with the 10.40am Saturdays only to Scarborough. The train is a mixture of Gresley, Thompson and BR Mk1 stock, mainly in carmine and cream, while the engine has gained a lipped chimney, rather than the ugly plain variety it carried previously, the first of the class so converted. Canyon-like Calton Road approaches the railway behind the metal bridge parapet. Photograph John Robertson, The Transport Treasury.

Top right. On 29 August 1953, A3 60096 PAPYRUS departs with the 10.05am to London St Pancras, the train later becoming 'The Waverley'. Named after the winner of the 1923 Derby, PAPYRUS entered service at Kings Cross in March 1929 as A1 2750. On 5 March 1935 the loco made a remarkable trial run between Kings Cross and Newcastle with six coaches and a dynamometer car, the return journey being accomplished in just under 232 minutes, with a record speed of 108mph. This proved that a four hour schedule to Newcastle was possible and set the scene for further developments of Gresley's Pacifics. After a couple of weeks at Haymarket in August 1937 and spells at Doncaster and Grantham, the engine moved from Kings Cross to Haymarket during July 1950 and remained there until transferred to St Margarets in December 1961. The new BR Mk 1 coaches are quite a contrast to the Thompson non-corridor standing below the Governor's House and Scottish Office. Photograph John Robertson, The Transport Treasury.

Right. The eastern throat of Waverley had an architectural backdrop unsurpassed at any other station in Britain. Piercing the skyline from left to right are the Scott Monument, the North British Hotel and the Governor's House of Calton Gaol. On a hot summer Sunday, 11 July 1954, A3 60080 DICK TURPIN draws three coaches out of one of the bays to add to the 9.40am from Glasgow Queen Street, which proceeded as the 11.30am (Sundays only) to Kings Cross. DICK TURPIN took the train forward to Newcastle where the Pacific was based for most of its life. As A1 2579, it was sent new to Heaton in November 1924, moved to Gateshead during August 1944 and back to Heaton in November 1945, remaining there until May 1960. As with many A3s, there had been frequent repaints prior to this view being taken. In this case, wartime black gave way to LNER Apple Green during August 1947, experimental BR Blue followed in October 1950 and Brunswick Green was applied in February 1952. Photograph John Robertson, The Transport Treasury.

Edinburgh citizens watching the huge heap of soil and building debris being piled up in the Waverley Valley during the late 1700s could not have envisaged the eventual appearance of The Mound. Firstly, it became an ideal platform for the dignified National Gallery of Scotland and the Royal Scottish Academy, the latter just visible on the right of this view. Then came the railway, tunnelling carefully through the detritus to avoid disturbing the noble foundations above. The Mound formed a perfect conclusion to the expanse of Waverley station in the west, even better than the natural barrier of Calton Hill at the east end. Having arrived one morning in April 1957, probably on an express from Glasgow Queen Street, A4 60031 GOLDEN PLOVER complements the classical background with its graceful lines. The stock has been removed and the engine is returning light to Haymarket shed. As only to be expected, the engine is in fine condition and even the buffers and coupling have been burnished. Photograph D.E. Beecroft, The Transport Treasury.

The Mound

'Another communication between the centre of the city and the New Town of Edinburgh has of late years been opened, by means of a mound of earth laid from the Lawnmarket across the North Loch. This mound was made passable for carriages in three years. It is above 800 feet in length. On the north it is 58 feet in height and on the south 92 feet. As it stands at present, it amounts to 435,250 cubic yards of travelled earth. It will be found that this mound contains 1,305,780 cart loads in all. It is said to have originated in the following manner. George Boyd, a shopkeeper in the Lawnmarket, who sold tartan, was extremely fond of visiting the New Town to observe the progress of the buildings by which the capital of his native country was about to be so remarkably extended and adorned. Finding it inconvenient to go round by the North Bridge, he prevailed with his neighbours to join with him in contributing a small sum of money to defray the expense of laying stepping stones across the North Loch, which, though drained, was still as at present a sort of swamp or morass. He next persuaded some of the persons employed in erecting houses in the New Town to convey to the same spot their rubbish, and the earth dug out in laying the foundations of their buildings. A tolerable footpath was thus made, which in the neighbourhood received the appellation of 'Geordie Boyd's Brig'. The advantage derived from an undertaking of the same sort, upon a greater scale, was soon perceived. Permission was granted to the builders in the New Town to deposit in this spot the whole earth and rubbish which they had occasion to remove. This was accepted as a privilege, because no place was found so convenient for that purpose. The magistrates obtained the authority of parliament for removing certain houses in the Lawnmarket to open a communication with the mound by a regular street and before he died, the original projector of the work had the mortification to see his own shop pulled down for this purpose.' From *The Beauties of Scotland* by Robert Forsyth, 1805.

This is a rather benevolent account of the construction of The Mound. At the time it must have been a very ugly sight, a huge heap of soil, stone and assorted building detritus blocking the valley and growing larger every week. It enraged the aesthetic feelings of many Edinburgh citizens, especially the academics and professionals, of which there were plenty. Time, nature and a touch of deliberate beautification mellowed the pile of debris and nowadays it is a positive asset to the city. Significant features in the enhancement of The Mound were the Royal Scottish Academy and the National Gallery of Scotland. Both buildings were designed by William Playfair (1789-1857), one of Edinburgh's most prominent architects and a passionate devotee of the classical style. His creations were largely instrumental in the city being dubbed 'The Athens of the North'.

The Mound and the National Gallery were, respectively, physical and architectural links with the New Town. The physical connection has already been described. After the 1707 Act of Union between Scotland and England, Edinburgh prospered. Unfortunately, even in the mid-1700s, it was still a congested, unhealthy place confined within its defensive walls. So the City Fathers devised the bold and imaginative plan to create a completely new town on the far side of North Loch, the drainage of which was part of the grand scheme. A young architect, James Craig, designed the

The west front of the National Gallery and the classical portal of Mound Tunnel below it were at their best on a sunny summer evening. That was the case on 22 June 1953. Flags and banners are out for the Edinburgh Festival, adding a touch of colour to the scene. B1 61261 leaves Waverley with the 6.25pm to Glasgow Queen Street, which originated at Kings Cross as the 10.10am. This particular B1 was very much a Glasgow engine, having been completed by the North British Loco Co in November 1947 prior to spending most of its life at Eastfield shed. Photograph John Robertson, The Transport Treasury.

first part of the New Town including the main thoroughfares, George Street and Princes Street. Thousands of houses were built in the classical style during this period of relentless construction which lasted well into the 1800s. It left Edinburgh with a wonderful legacy of dignified buildings, graceful squares and tree-lined crescents, in fact the largest area of Georgian architecture in Europe. William Playfair became involved with the New Town in its later stages and his talent was much in demand for buildings in other parts of the city, including of course, The Mound.

Top left. On the beautiful sunny evening of 20 June 1959, V3 67672 looks proud and determined as it leaves Mound Tunnel with a stopping train for Dunfermline. The Gresley engine and coaches blend beautifully with the Victorian tunnel portals and Georgian splendour above them. Originally allocated to the Great Eastern section, what was then V1 472 arrived at Stratford in November 1938. It was an early conversion to the higher pressure V3, this being accomplished during March 1943. The loco was one of those displaced from London by new L1 2-6-4Ts, but it readily found refuge at Dunfermline, minus the Westinghouse brake equipment required on the Great Eastern. 67672 ended its days at Dunfermline in December 1962. Photograph John Robertson, The Transport Treasury.

Bottom left. An afternoon train for Perth leaves Mound Tunnel on 5 July 1959 behind A3 60087 BLENHEIM, an unusual rostering for this particular working. The Pacific entered service in June 1930 as 2598 and was named after the winner of the 1930 Derby. Although BLENHEIM spent most of its first decade at Gateshead, it did have spells at Haymarket in 1937-38 and 1939-40. The engine took up permanent residence there during October 1941, but had a couple of years at St Margarets before withdrawal in October 1963. In 1954, 60087 was one of the A3s used in trials on expresses between Carlisle and Leeds via Ais Gill. Although the experiments were a success, regular use of ex-LNER Pacifics over the Settle & Carlisle route did not proceed at that stage. Photograph John Robertson, The Transport Treasury.

Late afternoon sunshine illuminates the foliage of Princes Street Gardens on 4 July 1959 as A2 60535 HORNETS BEAUTY arrives in Edinburgh with a summer Saturday relief from Aberdeen and Dundee made up of a variety of LMS-designed stock. The engine, named after the winner of the 1913 Portland Handicap, began its career at York in May 1948. Along with another two A2s from the same shed, 60535 moved north to Haymarket during November 1949 in exchange for three A2/2s, the rebuilt P2 2-8-2s, which were performing poorly on express passenger work in Scotland. After a spell at St Margarets from October 1961, there was a rather surprising transfer to Polmadie in September 1963, principally for replacing Stanier Pacifics on Glasgow-Carlisle duties. Withdrawal came in June 1965. Photograph John Robertson, The Transport Treasury.

Princes Street Gardens

'There are bright and temperate days, with soft air coming from the inland hills, military music sounding bravely from the hollow of the gardens, the flags all waving on the palaces of Princes Street, when I have seen the town through a sort of glory. On such a day, the valley wears a surprising air of festival. It seems as if it were a trifle too good to be true. It is what Paris ought to be. It has the scenic quality that would best set off a life of unthinking, open-air diversion. It was meant by nature for the realisation of the society of comic operas. And you could imagine, if the climate were but towardly, how all the world and his wife would flock into these gardens in the cool of the evening, to hear cheerful music, to sip pleasant drinks, to see the moon rise from behind Arthur's Seat and shine upon the spires and monuments and the green tree tops in the valley. Into no other city does the sight of the country enter so far; if you do not meet a butterfly, you shall certainly catch a glimpse of far away trees upon your walk.' From *Edinburgh, Picturesque Notes* by Robert Louis Stevenson, 1879.

The Gardens and the wonderful view of Edinburgh Castle from Princes Street did not come about by chance. With North Loch drained and the New Town taking shape, several public-spirited citizens became passionate about the aesthetics of the valley below the Old Town. Inevitably, they faced strenuous opposition from commercial interests eager to develop the newly available land. The radicals triumphed and in 1816 parliament prohibited buildings on the south side of Princes Street for all time. This statute, now in force for nearly two centuries, undoubtedly helped mould Edinburgh's unique character. Ironically, considering the nature of this book, the main threat to such verdant tranquillity was the extension of the Edinburgh & Glasgow Railway from Haymarket to North Bridge in 1846. Fortunately, room was made for the metals down in a cutting shrouded by trees. Even quadrupling following the opening of the Forth Bridge had no adverse effect and few people strolling along Princes Street were offended by drifting steam above the distant foliage. If the line through the Gardens had been denied, Edinburgh might still have termini at Haymarket and North Bridge with a connecting line through the suburbs and all the inconvenience that would imply.

Princes Street Gardens are in two parts, separated by The Mound. The West Gardens have Edinburgh's well known floral clock, the oldest in the world. There is also the Scottish American War Memorial, unveiled in 1927 and featuring a young soldier gazing intently towards the Castle. A massive boulder, donated by the people of Norway, is a reminder of friendships forged during World War Two when large numbers of Norwegians driven from their homeland found refuge and renewed hope in Scotland. In the East Gardens, between The Mound and Waverley Bridge, there is a memorial to the Royal Scots, the oldest regiment in the British Army, together with a statue of David Livingstone, the Scots doctor, explorer and missionary who famously encountered H.M. Stanley in the depths of Africa. Nearby, the famous 200ft spiky spire commemorates Sir Walter Scott, the novelist and patriot who was one of Edinburgh's favourite sons.

One of the taller buildings on Princes Street peeps through a gap in the trees above the smokebox of A3 60041 SALMON TROUT, which is running light from Haymarket to Waverley to take over an up East Coast working. The date is 15 August 1959, just two months after the engine received its double chimney. Note the transposition of numberplate and handrail, unusual, though not unique. Named after the winner of the 1924 St Leger, 2506 was one of the last batch of A3s to emerge from Doncaster Works and it took up residence at Haymarket in December 1934. SALMON TROUT moved to St Margarets in July 1960 where the loco found regular employment on goods traffic over the Waverley route. It was one of the last A3s in service, all of which were at St Margarets. The end for 60041 finally came in December 1965. Photograph John Robertson, The Transport Treasury.

The original double track through Princes Street Gardens opened in August 1846 and quadrupling was completed during the summer of 1895. Even with this many tracks, a shallow cutting and dense fringe of trees ensured that trains did not intrude on Edinburgh's favourite open space too much. In June 1956, a Suburban Outer Circle working coasts past the Gardens behind V1 67649. The loco, which was never converted to a higher pressure V3, went new to St Margarets as 2897 in December 1935 and remained there until withdrawn during July 1962. This view, looking towards the Caledonian Hotel, was taken from one of the lattice footbridges across the railway. Photograph John Robertson, The Transport Treasury.

With this leafy backdrop, those unacquainted with the western approach to Waverley would hardly guess that this is a railway in the heart of a major city. D49 62709 BERWICKSHIRE was built for fast passenger work, but it is most likely on empty coaching stock duties in this view. It is 25 June 1959 and the 4-4-0 is in its twilight days, withdrawal from Haymarket being only seven months away. This was after a respectably long career which began back in January 1928. Photograph John Robertson, The Transport Treasury.

Waverley Pacifics: A1s

Class A1 featured here is the type of Pacific familiar in BR years, rather than the earlier Gresley engines which became A3s. However, there is a connection, in fact one surrounded by controversy. When Edward Thompson succeeded Sir Nigel Gresley as Chief Mechanical Engineer in 1941, he had different ideas about locomotive design and believed in a limited number of standard classes. One of these was to be an express passenger 4-6-2 with 6ft 8in driving wheels, basically a development of the Gresley A4s. There was some delay while design work on the mixed traffic A2s proceeded, but plans emerged in 1944. For what seems to be emotional reasons, Thompson decided to rebuild the pioneering Gresley Pacific 4470 GREAT NORTHERN as a prototype, despite protestations. Reconstruction was almost total and, in common with his A2s, it had a somewhat strange appearance as a result of the bogie being placed forward of the outside cylinders, together with the long smokebox. The A1 appeared in 1945, was exhibited at Waverley in 1946 and had a brief spell at Haymarket

during 1947 while undergoing trials in Scotland. It was reclassified A1/1 the same year.

Thompson was eager to enlarge the class, but Doncaster drawing office took a long time over the necessary refinements, deliberately it has been suggested. A total of 39 A1s had been ordered or authorised when Arthur Peppercorn was appointed CME in 1946. He made several changes to the design, particularly at the front end, resulting in a much more conventional and attractive locomotive, like his version of the A2s. Ten more were ordered after Nationalisation and the whole batch of 49 was delivered between August 1948 and December 1949, Doncaster building 26 and Darlington 23. The A1s were welcomed

by sheds and crews alike, replacing engines well past their prime and taking the heaviest main line duties in their stride. Haymarket's complement were, famously, kept in immaculate condition by their regularly rostered drivers. Although the A1s appeared without names, they all acquired them eventually. Many were suggestions by members of the RCTS. The result was practically unique for one class, including racehorses, constituent companies of the LNER and locomotive superintendents. Others had bird names, some previously carried by A4s, or Scottish names associated with North British Atlantics and Scotts.

A1 Pacifics allocated to Haymarket.
Pre-1946 and Post-1946 LNER numbers in brackets. The BR number is shown first, even if the allocation to Haymarket was prior to it being carried.
60113=A1/1. 60114 to 60162=A1.
60113 (4470/113) GREAT NORTHERN: September 1947.
60152 HOLYROOD: July 1949-January 1951; March 1951-December 1952; June 1953-September 1963.
60159 BONNIE DUNDEE: November 1949-September 1963.
60160 AULD REEKIE: December 1949-January 1951; March 1951-September 1951; January 1952-September 1963.
60161 NORTH BRITISH: December 1949-January 1951; March 1951-September 1951; June 1953-September 1963.
60162 SAINT JOHNSTOUN: December 1949-September 1963.

Sent to St Margarets. (W) indicates withdrawn that month.
60152 HOLYROOD: September 1963-September 1964.
60159 BONNIE DUNDEE: September 1963-October 1963(W).
60160 AULD REEKIE: September 1963-December 1963(W).
60161 NORTH BRITISH: September 1963-October 1963(W).
60162 SAINT JOHNSTOUN: September 1963-October 1963(W).

It does not get much better than this! A1 60162 SAINT JOHNSTOUN, maintained in what can only be described as exhibition condition by its regular driver Willie Bain, leaves Waverley on 29 August 1953 with the up 'Queen of Scots' Pullman from Glasgow Queen Street to Kings Cross via Leeds Central. This Pacific would have been a wonderful ambassador for Haymarket shed had it ventured down to London, but the engine never worked a regular turn south of Newcastle. After completion at Doncaster in December 1949, 60162 went straight to Haymarket and stayed there virtually all of its life. In August 1951, following an overhaul at Doncaster when the livery was changed from BR blue to green, it took the name of C11 Atlantic 9901 which had been withdrawn in 1937. St Johnstoun is the old name for Perth. A story well worth repeating is that Willie Bain, allegedly, loved his engine more than his wife. He never denied the claim and eventually she did divorce him! Photograph John Robertson, The Transport Treasury.

A wonderful moment just east of Waverley on 10 April 1952. Volcanic rock, hefty retaining walls and the bastions of Calton Gaol form a raw backdrop to a display of elegance on the railway. A1 60159 BONNIE DUNDEE in blue livery and pristine condition hauls brand new BR Standard stock in carmine and cream from Craigentinny carriage sidings to form an Aberdeen service. The engine went new from Doncaster to Haymarket in November 1949 and remained there until a matter of weeks before its demise. In July 1951 it took the name of C11 Atlantic 9869, withdrawn back in October 1935. Perhaps contrary to expectation, BONNIE DUNDEE does not celebrate the city on the Tay, but refers to Viscount Dundee, a prominent Royalist soldier. 60159 was repainted in Brunswick green at the end of 1952, one of the last A1s to receive this livery. It was languishing at St Margarets when condemned in October 1963. Photograph John Robertson, The Transport Treasury.

Gateshead shed was well known for the scruffy appearance, yet mechanically-sound condition, of its Pacifics. Typical was A1 60150 WILLBROOK, waiting to back on to a southbound express at Waverley on 25 July 1953. It was outshopped in Brunswick green during March 1952, just sixteenth months previously. The cylinder casing does need a bit of attention, having taken a swipe. This A1 was completed at Darlington in June 1949 and was named after the winner of the 1914 Doncaster Cup in January 1951, when the livery was changed from LNER green to BR blue. 60150 spent most of its life at Gateshead and often worked the 'Night Scotsman' from Newcastle to London and back, followed by an out and home trip to Edinburgh. Photograph John Robertson, The Transport Treasury.

This rather unusual view of Waverley was taken on 17 September 1949 and features A1 60152 which only emerged new from Darlington Works two months previously. It was the last of the class to wear LNER apple green livery, the repaint in blue being completed during June 1951. At the same time 60152 was named HOLYROOD, commemorating C11 Atlantic 9904 and, of course, the Royal Palace and former abbey in Edinburgh. Here, the A1 is at platform 11 on a Glasgow Queen Street express, but less conventional journeys lay ahead. From January to March 1951 and during the first six months of 1953, the Pacific went to Polmadie and worked out of Glasgow Central to Carlisle and even Crewe. Its stay there also brought it to, of all places, Edinburgh Princes Street station! Otherwise, it remained a Haymarket engine until September 1963. Photograph Dr D.M. Alexander, The Transport Treasury.

In time-honoured fashion, a father has taken his children to the end of the platform to have a look at the engine, probably before boarding the train. It is 21 May 1955 and A1 60115 MEG MERRILIES is in charge of the up 'Flying Scotsman'. This was a regular turn for a Gateshead A1, out to Edinburgh with an early morning service, then back to Newcastle with the 10.00am express. 60115 was completed at Doncaster in September 1948 and on the 27th of that month worked the first up 'Tees-Tyne Pullman' to Kings Cross. In June 1950, when blue livery was applied, the engine took the name of D29 Scott 9243. It was at Gateshead until November 1960, then spent the last two years of its life at Copley Hill shed in Leeds. Photograph P. Wilson, The Transport Treasury.

A stiff breeze coming in from the Firth of Forth swirls smoke and steam around A2/1 60510 ROBERT THE BRUCE as it leaves Waverley with the 10.05am for London St Pancras on an unknown date in the early 1950s. One of the four engines built instead of V2s, it left Darlington Works as 3699 in January 1945 and went to Haymarket the following March. At the time, small smoke deflectors were fitted either side of the chimney, the larger ones coming later. In April 1948 the engine was named after the Scottish king who defeated the English at the Battle of Bannockburn in 1314. Although never allocated top link work, 60510 was used on express passenger and goods trains to Aberdeen, Newcastle and Carlisle. It was withdrawn from St Margarets in November 1960, four months after moving from Haymarket. Photograph John Robertson, The Transport Treasury.

Waverley Pacifics: A2s

The class here is the rather varied set of forty Pacifics which materialised during the 1940s, not the five A2s of North Eastern Railway origin which had become extinct by 1937. In view of the economic constraints of wartime, Thompson's standardisation and simplification policy was logical. After all, Gresley's large engines were quite expensive to maintain, especially when it came to the valve gear. In addition to a 6ft 8in express passenger type, Thompson wanted a mixed traffic design with 6ft 2in driving wheels and this project was given priority. A start was made in 1943-44 by rebuilding the six P2 2-8-2s, which the new CME seems to have detested. They were the first engines to have the ungainly front end and were simply designated A2 until reclassified A2/2 in 1945. Numbers and names from the P2s were retained. Initially, the rebuilds returned to express passenger duties between Edinburgh and Aberdeen, but were soon used almost exclusively on fast goods trains. All of them were transferred from Haymarket to English sheds at the end of 1949. The first new mixed traffic 4-6-2s, classified A2/1, appeared in 1944-45 and were basically a Pacific version of the V2. In fact, these four engines were built at Darlington instead of the last 2-6-2s and even took their numbers. Names suggested by the RCTS were applied in 1946-48. Three of them spent most of their time at Haymarket and worked express passenger and goods traffic to Dundee, Aberdeen, Newcastle and Carlisle, albeit not in the top link.

By 1945, no less than 43 standard 6ft 2in Pacifics based on the rebuilt P2s had been authorised. Fifteen were constructed in 1946-47, the first of them named EDWARD THOMPSON after its designer and the rest after racehorses. The new engines were classified A2 until 1947, when they became A2/3. Haymarket's 60519 HONEYWAY was the only one based in Scotland, working over all the main lines out of Edinburgh on express passenger, parcels, fish, meat and general goods trains. Nevertheless, Gateshead and Heaton A2/3s regularly ventured north of the border. When Thompson retired in 1946, Peppercorn's influence came to the forefront and it seems that some redesigning had already been done on the quiet. The more conventional front end even incorporated a single chimney, possibly an attempt to recreate the good looks of the Gresley era, although the policy was eventually reversed. Fifteen engines, once again taking the A2 classification, were built in 1947-48, the remainder being cancelled pending an assessment of motive power requirements by BR. Haymarket's A2s were used on all manner of express traffic, especially over the Aberdeen road where their impressive power and acceleration proved particularly useful.

Thompson's arrangement for the front end is clearly shown in this view of A2/3 60521 WATLING STREET, departing from Waverley with the 10.30am to Newcastle on 24 March 1951. The train conveyed parcels as well as passengers, as shown by the first two vehicles. Doncaster-built 521, named after the winner of the 1942 Derby, was new to Gateshead in May 1947. The uninteresting plain chimney, relieved only by a narrow beading round the lip, soon gave way to a cast variety with considerably more aesthetic merit. WATLING STREET moved across the Tyne to Heaton in May 1960 and was withdrawn in November 1962 after a year at Tweedmouth shed. Photograph John Robertson, The Transport Treasury.

A2 Pacifics allocated to Haymarket.
Pre-1946 and Post-1946 LNER numbers in brackets. The BR number is shown first, even if the allocation to Haymarket was prior to it being carried.
60501 to 60506=A2/2. 60507 to 60510=A2/1. 60500 and 60511 to 60524=A2/3. 60525 to 60539=A2.
60501 (2001/501) COCK O' THE NORTH: September 1944-October 1944; September 1949-November 1949.
60502 (2002/502) EARL MARISCHAL: September 1949-November 1949.
60503 (2003/503) LORD PRESIDENT: December 1944; March 1945-April 1945; May 1945-November 1949.
60504 (2004/504) MONS MEG: November 1944-January 1950.
60505 (2005/505) THANE OF FIFE: April 1943-December 1949.
60506 (2006/506) WOLF OF BADENOCH: May 1944-April 1949; May 1949-November 1949.
60507 (3696/507) HIGHLAND CHIEFTAIN: December 1949-July 1955; August 1955-July 1960.
60509 (3698/509) WAVERLEY: March 1945-August 1960.
60510 (3699/510) ROBERT THE BRUCE: March 1945-July 1960.
60519 (519) HONEYWAY: February 1947-October 1961.
60529 (E529) PEARL DIVER: February 1948-October 1961.
60530 (E530) SAYAJIRAO: January 1950-October 1961.
60532 BLUE PETER: November 1949-January 1951.
60534 IRISH ELEGANCE: November 1949-November 1961.
60535 HORNET'S BEAUTY: November 1949-October 1961.
60536 TRIMBUSH: November 1949-November 1961; May 1962-October 1962.
60537 BACHELOR'S BUTTON: January 1951-November 1961.

A2s allocated to St Margarets (W) indicates withdrawn that month.
60507 HIGHLAND CHIEFTAIN: July 1960-December 1960(W).
60510 ROBERT THE BRUCE: July 1960-November 1960(W).
60519 HONEYWAY: October 1961-December 1962(W).
60522 STRAIGHT DEAL: December 1962-September 1963.
60524 HERRINGBONE: December 1962.
60529 PEARL DIVER: October 1961-December 1962(W).
60530 SAYAJIRAO: October 1961-September 1963.
60534 IRISH ELEGANCE: November 1961-December 1962(W).
60535 HORNETS BEAUTY: October 1961-September 1963.
60536 TRIMBUSH: November 1961-May 1962; October 1962-December 1962(W).
60537 BACHELORS BUTTON: November 1961-December 1962(W).

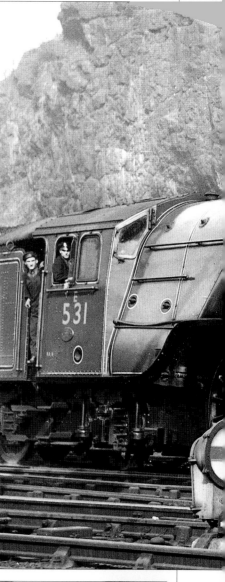

Top right. Brand new E531 BAHRAM is a very fine sight as it poses below Calton Hill ready to take over an East Coast express, probably in April 1948. From March 1948 to August 1949 the A2 was at Gateshead, but it then migrated to Aberdeen where it stayed until condemned in December 1962. LNER apple green livery gave way to BR green in June 1949, but the single chimney remained until the end. The engine was named after the Aga Khan's very successful racehorse which won the Derby, 2000 Guineas and St Leger in 1935. Photograph J.R. Patterson, The Transport Treasury.

Below. On a warm and sunny 3 July 1954, the up 'Heart of Midlothian' leaves Edinburgh for Kings Cross behind Peppercorn A2 60529 PEARL DIVER. The engine and crew went as far as Newcastle, then returned on the balancing down working. These trains were known to Haymarket men as 'The Diners'. PEARL DIVER, celebrating the winner of the 1947 Derby, was an Edinburgh engine all its life. Haymarket took delivery of E529 from Doncaster Works in February 1948 and withdrawal after just over a year at St Margarets came in 1962. In common with all but the last member of the class, it originally had a single chimney, but this was replaced when a double blast pipe was fitted in September 1949, one of six A2s so treated. A cast version came later. Photograph The Transport Treasury.

Certain A2s spent some time fitted with Diagram 117 boilers of Thompson design, identified by a circular dome further forward, rather than the streamlined cover of the later 118 type. 60537 BACHELORS BUTTON ran in this condition from 1958 to 1961, as seen here on 4 July 1959 while getting an Aberdeen express underway. 60537 went new to Copley Hill in June 1948, moved to New England during January 1949, then Aberdeen in July 1949. Here it proved to be a poor steamer and was sent to Haymarket in return for double-chimney A2 60532 BLUE PETER during January 1951. Although hardly Edinburgh's most popular Pacific, BACHELORS BUTTON was based in the city until withdrawn during December 1962, having spent its final year at St Margarets. Photograph John Robertson, The Transport Treasury.

On the beautiful summer afternoon of 29 August 1953, 60037 HYPERION makes a determined start from Waverley as it leaves Mound Tunnel with an Edinburgh-Perth express. Originally 2502 and named after the winner of the 1933 Derby and St Leger, the A3 went new to Haymarket in July 1934. The Pacific stayed there until November 1961, apart from March 1938 to March 1939 when allocated to St Margarets, specifically for working the 12 noon express to Carlisle and the 4.25am to Perth. At Haymarket it gained an unenviable reputation as the worst A3 allocated there. However, the well-known driver and author Norman McKillop was given the Pacific when his beloved SPEARMINT was in the shops. As something of an engine 'doctor', he diagnosed its faults and turned the loco sufficiently to make it fit enough to haul the Royal Train a few months later. HYPERION finished its days at St Margarets in December 1963. Photograph John Robertson, The Transport Treasury.

Waverley Pacifics: A3s

Gresley's non-streamlined Pacifics, one of the most celebrated locomotive types in British railway history, were a familiar sight at Waverley for over forty years. Furthermore, they were very popular with Haymarket men who did not usually take kindly to English engines. Although the story of these 4-6-2s has been told many times, it is well worth summarising in the context of Waverley. The first two A1s, with 6ft 8in driving wheels and 180lb sq in boiler pressure, were built for the Great Northern Railway in 1922. They were designed to haul express passenger trains weighing up to 600 tons, an unprecedented load for one engine. A further ten were ordered from Doncaster Works by the GN and these entered service with the LNER during 1923. Towards the end of that year, Waverley saw its first Pacifics on services from Newcastle. Forty more appeared in 1924-25 and the first five, part of a batch of twenty built by the North British Loco Co in Glasgow, were allocated to Haymarket. These were specifically for Newcastle workings previously handled by North Eastern engines based in Edinburgh, but they also had trips to Glasgow. Although the A1s proved highly competent at hauling very heavy loads over the East Coast main line, they had deficiencies which were shown up by the famous exchange trials with Great Western Castle 4-6-0s in 1925. As a result, Gresley modified the valve gear and in 1927-28 five were fitted with 220lb sq in boilers.

These upgraded engines were reclassified A3.

Exciting times lay ahead for the LNER. On 1 May 1928 the first non-stop runs of the 'Flying Scotsman' departed simultaneously at 10.00am from Waverley and Kings Cross, an occasion which generated a huge amount of interest. Haymarket had made a large unofficial headboard for A3 2580 SHOTOVER on the southbound working and this feature was subsequently adopted by the LNER for expresses and even more widely by BR. The A3s were so successful that 27 new ones entered service between 1928 and 1935. During 1928, Pacifics were allocated to Carlisle Canal and worked into Edinburgh over the Waverley route. Haymarket acquired another three in 1930 and workings to Dundee and Aberdeen commenced. Five of the final batch of nine went to Haymarket in 1934-35, but within a year attention had turned to the streamlined A4s. From early 1938 to a reorganisation of Edinburgh duties in late 1940, St Margarets had a succession of A1s and A3s for its Carlisle duties. Conversion of the remaining A1s to A3s commenced in 1939 but was not finished until 1948. By 1951 the principal East Coast expresses were largely handled by A4s and new A1s, so the A3s tended to gravitate to secondary and shorter distance main line workings. Earlier, there had been strong trade union representations

about the difficulty of sighting colour light signals from right-hand drive Pacifics. Haymarket drivers had always disliked this arrangement anyway, so four left-hand drive A3s from England were exchanged for existing residents during 1951. The A3s were probably at their best towards the end of their careers when double blast pipes and chimneys were fitted in 1958-59. After a long and happy association with Edinburgh, it was appropriate that the three A3s which remained in service during 1965 were at St Margarets.

For most of its life a Tyneside resident, 60080 DICK TURPIN leaves Waverley with the 9.40am Sundays only Glasgow Queen Street - London Kings Cross on 11 July 1954. The name was a bit of an enigma as it certainly did not relate to a classic racehorse, although there was an equine connection! As A1 2579, the engine went brand new from North British Loco Co in Glasgow to Heaton in November 1924. It became an A3 at the end of 1942, the peak year for conversions following a solitary example during 1939 and a more determined start in 1941. Back at Waverley in 1954, the summer air was so clear that even at this distance the North British Hotel clock confirms a punctual 11.30am departure, bearing in mind that it is two minutes fast. Photograph John Robertson, The Transport Treasury.

In the familiar setting of Princes Street Gardens just west of Mound Tunnel, 60043 BROWN JACK sets off with an Aberdeen express. The date is 4 July 1959 and the A3 is seen with its double chimney, which had been fitted five months previously. All the class received these in 1958-59, apart from 60097 which had been modified earlier. BROWN JACK, named after a famous racehorse which won the Queen Alexandra Stakes from 1929 to 1934, was the very last A3 to be built. It went new to Haymarket as 2508 in February 1935 and stayed there until November 1961. The Great Northern style tender was allocated to the Pacific in March 1938, but from April 1935 to April 1937 it was coupled to a corridor tender for the non-stop runs. Photograph John Robertson, The Transport Treasury.

A3 Pacifics allocated to Haymarket. Pre-1946 and Post-1946 LNER numbers in brackets. The BR number is shown first, even if the allocation to Haymarket was prior to it being carried.

60035 (2500/35) WINDSOR LAD: July 1934-March 1937; April 1937-May 1961; August 1961.
60037 (2502/37) HYPERION: July 1934-March 1938; March 1939-November 1961.
60040 (2505/40) CAMERONIAN: October 1934-November 1936.
60041 (2506/41) SALMON TROUT: December 1934-July 1960.
60043 (2508/43) BROWN JACK: February 1935-November 1961.
60057 (2556/57) ORMONDE: March 1939; December 1940-March 1943; April 1943-April 1961; May 1961-December 1961.
60062 (2561/62) MINORU: April 1945-May 1945.
60064 (2563/64) WILLIAM WHITELAW (later TAGALIE): August 1924-April 1935; December 1940-July 1950.
60065 (2564/65) KNIGHT OF THISTLE: August 1924-February 1937; December 1941-July 1950.
60066 (2565/66) MERRY HAMPTON: August 1924-May 1928; July 1928-October 1930; August 1931-December 1931; February 1941-August 1950.
60067 (2566/67) LADAS: August 1924-August 1930; November 1940-July 1950.
60068 (2567/68) SIR VISTO: September 1924-August 1930.
60074 (2573/74) HARVESTER: April 1928-July 1928; April 1937-February 1938.
60079 (2578/79) BAYARDO: September 1937-January 1938.
60081 (2580/81) SHOTOVER: April 1928-September 1928.
60087 (2598/87) BLENHEIM: October 1937-February 1938; March 1939-July 1940; October 1941-July 1960; December 1960-December 1961.
60088 (2599/88) BOOK LAW: October 1937-January 1938.
60089 (2743/89) FELSTEAD: February 1951-December 1960.
60090 (2744/90) GRAND PARADE: July 1937-March 1938; July 1950-November 1960.
60091 (2745/91) CAPTAIN CUTTLE: October 1928.
60093 (2747/93) CORONACH: March 1939-January 1941.
60094 (2748/94) COLORADO: December 1947-December 1961.
60096 (2750/96) PAPYRUS: August 1937-September 1937; July 1950-December 1961.
60097 (2751/97) HUMORIST: July 1950-January 1954; February 1954-December 1961.
60098 (2752/98) SPION COP: January 1938-February 1938; August 1950-January 1963.
60099 (2795/99) CALL BOY: April 1930-January 1940; October 1940-January 1963.
60100 (2796/100) SPEARMINT: May 1930-April 1937; March 1938-July 1938; December 1940-January 1963.
60101 (2797/101) CICERO: June 1930-February 1937; October 1940-January 1963.

A3s allocated to St Margarets. Pre-1946 LNER numbers in brackets where appropriate, although the BR number is shown first, even if the allocation to Haymarket was prior to it being carried. (W) indicates withdrawn that month.

60037 (2502) HYPERION: March 1938-March 1939; November 1961-December 1963(W).
60041 SALMON TROUT: July 1960-December 1965(W).
60042 SINGAPORE: October 1963-July 1964(W).
60043 BROWN JACK: November 1961-May 1964(W).
60052 PRINCE PALATINE: June 1963-January 1966(W).
60053 SANSOVINO: April 1963-May 1963(W).
60057 (2556) ORMONDE: March 1939-February 1940; December 1961-October 1963(W).
60064 (2563) WILLIAM WHITELAW (later TAGALIE): July 1938-January 1940.
60067 (2566) LADAS: January 1940-November 1940.
60068 (2567) SIR VISTO: November 1938-February 1940.
60077 THE WHITE KNIGHT: June 1963-July 1964.
60087 BLENHEIM: June 1960-December 1960; December 1961-October 1963(W).
60089 FELSTEAD: December 1960-October 1963(W).
60090 GRAND PARADE: December 1960-June 1962.
60094 COLORADO: December 1961-June 1962.
60096 PAPYRUS: December 1961-July 1963(W).
60097 HUMORIST: December 1961-August 1963(W).
60098 (2752) SPION COP: February 1938-March 1938; January 1963-October 1963(W).
60099 (2795) CALL BOY: January 1940-October 1940; January 1963-October 1963(W).
60100 SPEARMINT: January 1963-June 1965(W).
60101 (2797) CICERO: February 1940-October 1940; January 1963-April 1963(W).

Platform 20 at Waverley, primarily intended for local services on the South Suburban line, hosted this Saturday express for Kings Cross on 3 July 1954. In charge is 60094 COLORADO, named after the winner of the 1926 2000 Guineas. As only to be expected, the Haymarket engine is in fine condition. It had been transferred to Edinburgh during December 1947, but was no stranger to the city as a result of its allocation to Carlisle Canal in April 1929 for Waverley route duties. From new in December 1928, A3 2748 went to Doncaster, then Kings Cross before moving north. At the end of its career, 60094 was at St Rollox from June 1962 to February 1964 for working Glasgow - Aberdeen expresses. Photograph John Robertson. The Transport Treasury.

Waning sunlight and lengthening shadows mellow the Old Town on an autumn evening in 1956 as 60097 HUMORIST, named after the winner of the 1921 Derby, waits to leave platform 14 with a Glasgow express. This particular A3 was unique in having large smoke deflectors, which were fitted in 1947. It was not the first time that the loco had been involved in trials addressing the problem of drifting smoke. During 1932-33, a dual chimney, vanes and cut-away sections of the smokebox featured in various air-lifting experiments. Then in 1937 a Kylchap double blast pipe and chimney were fitted. New as A3 2751 in April 1929, HUMORIST went to Kings Cross during October 1946 and made 58 consecutive trips on the 'Yorkshire Pullman', newly restored after the war. It was a Haymarket engine from July 1950 to December 1961. Photograph, The Transport Treasury.

Without wishing to detract from the days of glory at Haymarket, it is perhaps worth recording that there were less glamorous moments. In the Spring of 1961, filthy A3 60057 ORMONDE leaves platform 2 with the lightly-loaded 3.43pm slow to Berwick and in this case the external appearance of the engine reflected its mechanical condition. Indeed, several Haymarket drivers had complained about the state of 60057. As a result, it had a general overhaul at Doncaster Works, emerging in September 1961, complete with German-style smoke deflectors. Afterwards, ORMONDE proved one of Haymarket's best A3s, but it only stayed there until the following December when St Margarets became its new home. As A1 2556, named after the winner of the 1886 Derby, 2000 Guineas and St Leger, the Pacific went new to Grantham in February 1925, but had no less than twelve changes of shed during its lifetime. There was a stint at St Margarets from March 1939 to February 1940 for Carlisle workings, then the lengthy stay at Haymarket from April 1943. 60057 was withdrawn in October after a creditable 38½ years service. Photograph The Transport Treasury.

Summer 1937 was a spectacular time for brand new A4 4492 DOMINION OF NEW ZEALAND. The engine went new to Kings Cross in June 1937, then took up residence at Haymarket during July. From the 18th to the 27th of that month, it worked the non-stop 'Flying Scotsman' every day, displacing A1s and A3s. Then there were 44 days on ordinary expresses between the capital cities, followed by eight more on the 'Flying Scotsman'. In all, 4492 worked 62 trains between Kings Cross and Edinburgh that summer, 52 of them consecutively and a record at the time. The A4 went to Kings Cross again in March 1938 and was withdrawn from there as 60013 in April 1963. In this view, DOMINION OF NEW ZEALAND is seen at Waverley during that memorable summer of 1937. Photograph K J McDonald, The Transport Treasury.

Waverley Pacifics: A4s

For nearly seventy years, Gresley's streamlined Pacifics have been among the most famous locomotives in Britain and, indeed, the world. Virtually everything that can be said about them has already been published, but their glamorous and almost lifelong association with Haymarket and Waverley justifies a brief reminder here. In spring 1934, with the first P2 nearing completion, Gresley instructed Doncaster to design a Pacific version of the 2-8-2s, the original outline being very similar to its predecessors. At the time there was a lot of interest in high-speed services and the spectacular trial run with A3 2750 PAPYRUS from Kings Cross to Newcastle and back proved that very fast running over long distances was feasible. The LNER therefore decided to inaugurate a prestigious high-speed service to Newcastle in the autumn of 1935. Motive power would be provided by new A4s with 6ft 8in driving wheels

and a boiler pressure of no less than 250lb sq in. Four were ordered in March 1935 and gradually the distinctive streamlined shape evolved. With their revolutionary outline, three-tone grey livery and melodious chime whistles, these new Pacifics commanded a lot of attention. They were also very fast. Even on the trial run to Grantham in September 1935, 2509 SILVER LINK reached 112mph, an astonishing debut.

The 'Silver Jubilee' to Newcastle began in October 1935 and proved very popular. By the end of the year it was realised that the A4s had such a reserve of power that they were just as capable of hauling heavy trains at moderate speed as lightweight ones at high speed. Consequently, another 31 were ordered in 1936, for general duties as well as two more fast luxury trains. One of these was the London-Edinburgh 'Coronation' which commenced in July 1937. At the same time, A4s took over the non-stop

summer 'Flying Scotsman'. The pinnacle of achievement in terms of speed came on 3 July 1938, of course, when 4468 MALLARD reached 125mph. With World War Two imminent, the luxury high speed trains ceased at the end of August 1939 and a glorious era for the railways was over.

Waverley saw its first A4 in November 1935 when 2510 QUICKSILVER made an appearance, then from December 1937 Gateshead's 2511 SILVER KING was a regular visitor on trains from Newcastle. Haymarket received its first streamlined Pacific in December 1936 and was home to six of them by the following summer. A maximum of ten was reached in March 1938 but the allocation stabilised at seven from 1941. Most of their work involved journeys to Newcastle, Dundee and Glasgow, although Haymarket also had its share of turns to King's Cross on the pre-war 'Coronation', the non-

With all the smoke, steam and fragmented stark shapes, it was almost apocalypse in this view of Waverley early in 1937. Centre of attention is 4483 KINGFISHER, Haymarket's first A4, which arrived at the shed in December 1936. The streamlined Pacific, seen here in green with the aesthetically disastrous all black smokebox, was on an express for Glasgow, or maybe Aberdeen. In July 1937 the engine moved to Kings Cross, but returned to Haymarket the following January wearing the far more satisfactory LNER blue. In common with many other Pacifics, there was then a succession of black, blue, purple and blue liveries before stability came with Brunswick green in March 1952. 60024 KINGFISHER remained at Haymarket until September 1963, then had spells at Dalry Road and St Margarets in Edinburgh before being transferred to Aberdeen in April 1966. On 13 September 1966, it headed the 5.15pm to Glasgow Buchanan Street and the 8.25am return working the next day, the last A4 to haul an ordinary timetabled passenger train. Photograph Dr R A Read, The Transport Treasury.

The 10.50am Sunday departure from Edinburgh to Kings Cross
on 11 July 1954 is about ten minutes late according to the hotel
clock, but no doubt Haymarket's 60027 MERLIN, in pristine
condition, will make up the deficit by Newcastle. The air is clear
and the sunshine bright as MERLIN bids farewell to Scott's
spiky monument and the dour ramparts of Calton Hill on one
of its regular trips to England. Later in the day, the Pacific will
return to its home depot where it was delivered new as 4486 in
March 1937. After a spell at St Rollox from May 1962 to September
1964, the engine spent a year at St Margarets before its demise.
Photograph John Robertson, The Transport Treasury.

stop 'Flying Scotsman' and the 'Elizabethan' which was introduced in 1953. During the war and after nationalisation there were regular trips to Aberdeen. Wartime conditions meant that locomotives throughout the country were worked exceptionally hard and became generally run-down, but Haymarket made every effort to keep its A4s on regular duties and as well maintained as possible. After the war there was a complete reorganisation of crew and locomotive rostering at Haymarket and, as far as the Edinburgh shed was concerned, another glorious era began. Most Pacifics had regular sets of men, notably the six A4s in No.1 Link. They were kept in superb mechanical condition and their external appearance was legendary. Although the streamliners rarely ventured on to the Waverley route, they regularly graced the suburban terminus at Corstorphine and the grandiose confines of Leith Central. With the influx of main line diesels, the A4s moved away from Edinburgh, many for a dignified finale at Aberdeen.

A4 Pacifics allocated to Haymarket. Pre-1946 and Post-1946 LNER numbers in brackets. The BR number is shown first, even if the allocation to Haymarket was prior to it being carried.

60004 (4462/4) WILLIAM WHITELAW: July 1941-June 1962; September 1962-June 1963.
60009 (4488/9) UNION OF SOUTH AFRICA: June 1937-May 1962.
60011 (4490/11) EMPIRE OF INDIA: March 1938-June 1962.
60012 (4491/12) COMMONWEALTH OF AUSTRALIA: June 1937-September 1963.
60013 (4492/13) DOMINION OF NEW ZEALAND: July 1937-March 1938.
60023 (4482/23) GOLDEN EAGLE: January 1938-August 1941.
60024 (4483/24) KINGFISHER: December 1936-July 1937; January 1938-April 1939; May 1939-September 1963.
60025 (4484/25) FALCON: February 1937-March 1939.
60026 (4485/26) MILES BEEVOR: February 1937-September 1937; January 1938-March 1939.
60027 (4486/27) MERLIN: March 1937-May 1962.
60028 (4487/28) WALTER K WHIGHAM: February 1938-March 1939; April 1939-May 1939.
60031 (4497/31) GOLDEN PLOVER: October 1937-February 1962.

A4s allocated to St Margarets (W) indicates withdrawn that month. All but one moved on to Aberdeen.

60005 SIR CHARLES NEWTON: October 1963-November 1963.
60006 SIR RALPH WEDGWOOD: October 1963-May 1964.
60007 SIR NIGEL GRESLEY: October 1963-July 1964.
60016 SILVER KING: October 1963-November 1963.
60019 BITTERN: October 1963-November 1963.
60023 GOLDEN EAGLE: October 1963-May 1964.
60024 KINGFISHER: December 1963-April 1966.
60026 MILES BEEVOR: October 1963-April 1964.
60027 MERLIN: September 1964-September 1965(W).
60034 LORD FARINGDON: October 1963-May 1964.

A delightful cameo at Waverley on 17 June 1949. 60033 SEAGULL is eager to get 'The Capitals Limited' for Kings Cross on the move, but its driver in flat cap and workaday footplate wear finds time to spend with a mother and child, leaning forward, maybe to reassure the infant that the beast behind him poses no threat. Apart from a break at Grantham between April 1944 and March 1948, SEAGULL was always a London engine, delivered to Kings Cross as 4902 in June 1938 and withdrawn from Top Shed in December 1962. In this view it is in LNER blue, but experimental BR blue was applied the following year. Brunswick green, which suited these engines so well, came in the summer of 1952. Photograph M.N. Bland, The Transport Treasury.

At the height of summer, the sun stays out late in Scotland and was still bright enough to illuminate sparkling 60012 COMMONWEALTH OF AUSTRALIA as it reached Edinburgh late in the evening with an express from Kings Cross during July 1954. Because of the gradient from St Margarets, the A4 is still working hard as it draws its train of carmine and cream Thompson and BR Standard coaches out of Calton Tunnel over the last few hundred yards to Waverley. On the right is Waverley goods depot. The Pacific went new to Haymarket in June 1937 as 4491 and soon made its mark when it hauled the inaugural Kings Cross - Edinburgh working of 'The Coronation' on 3 July 1937. At the time, this was the fastest schedule for any train in Britain. 60012 finished its days at Aberdeen in August 1964. Photograph John Robertson, The Transport Treasury.

It was an overcast summer Saturday in Edinburgh, but 60031 GOLDEN PLOVER was still a sparkling sight as it made a determined start with the 10.20am relief to the up 'Flying Scotsman' on 25 July 1953. The train, unofficially known as the 'Junior Scotsman', left Waverley at 10.10am on weekdays but was ten minutes later on Saturdays and started from Glasgow Queen Street at 8.35am. This particular A4 had a wonderful phase of its career soon after it was allocated to Haymarket as 4497 in October 1937. In the spring of 1939 it worked 39 consecutive round trips on 'The Coronation', accumulating 15,327 miles in just over six weeks. At the other end of its life, it spent February 1962 to October 1965 at St Rollox for the Glasgow Buchanan Street-Aberdeen expresses. Photograph John Robertson, The Transport Treasury.

A view epitomising the glamorous days at Haymarket, taken on 2 March 1952. Willie Bain's A1 60162 SAINT JOHNSTOUN glistens in the shed yard, its handrails, smokebox door handles, buffers and even couplings scoured to perfection. The cab fittings would have been equally spotless. Here, the engine still has the original plain chimney. Passing by is A2 60534 IRISH ELEGANCE on a stopping train to Dundee. Named after the winner of the 1919 Royal Hunt Cup, it was completed by Doncaster Works in April 1948 and was at York until transferred to Haymarket during November 1949. This was one of the A2s which retained its single chimney until the end. Withdrawal came in December 1962 after a year at St Margarets. Dominating the scene is Haymarket's mechanical coaling plant, which was an enormous improvement. Photograph John Robertson, The Transport Treasury.

Glamour Boys

When the Edinburgh & Glasgow Railway opened in 1842, an engine shed was provided just west of Haymarket station, the eastern terminus of the line. It gradually increased in importance following the extension to North Bridge, take-over of the E&G by the North British, the opening of new lines and development of the Lothian coalfield. Completion of the Forth Bridge in 1891 resulted in a huge increase in traffic and it was obvious that the somewhat antiquated depot would not be able to cope with any more locomotives. Therefore, the North British acquired a substantial area of farmland alongside the main line north of Merchiston and an eight-road, double-ended straight shed was constructed, together with a turntable, coaling bank and numerous sidings. The new shed opened in 1894, a contemporary of the quadrupling of the route to Saughton Junction where the Glasgow and Fife routes diverged. Although it was nearly ¾ mile west of the facilities it replaced, the depot kept

the name Haymarket. For thirty years, its principal role was to provide a wide range of motive power for all manner of duties on the North British system north and west of Edinburgh, although from 1901 the North Eastern rented accommodation for main line engines on workings to and from Newcastle. Immediately after the Grouping of 1923, the LNER decided to make Haymarket the principal depot for express passenger turns. There were still rosters for local passenger, goods and shunting work, but the legendary charisma of Haymarket as a Top Link shed had been initiated.

An interesting insight into how the shed had to be improved for its new role is revealed by a series of LNER missives. On 21 February 1929, well after the first Pacifics had been allocated to Haymarket, it was reported that the coaling stage was in a very unsatisfactory condition and needed an outlay of £250 to make it last for a few more years. It would then require renewal at a much heavier cost.

For an estimated £15,632 a mechanical coaler could be installed, together with a 70ft turntable in place of the existing 50ft table and an additional ashpit in view of the increasing number of engines with drop grates. A decision was deferred for two months, longer as it turned out. The 70ft turntable and mechanical coaler were approved on 27 June 1929 and 25 July 1929 respectively at a total cost of £16,481. No doubt the ashpit received official sanction as well, for on 23 April 1931 attention turned to the steam grab crane which had proved so successful at Eastfield and Parkhead sheds in Glasgow. Sentinel self-propelled ash crane 773066 duly entered service at Haymarket in January 1932. It provided an interesting contrast to the streamlined Pacifics which arrived a few years later.

The post-war reorganisation of Haymarket rosters, dedicating individual locomotives to specific crews, was embraced enthusiastically by the men. There was rivalry, not only

Although this is a familiar photograph, it is well worth repeating as a look back at those exciting early days of Pacifics at Haymarket. The view probably dates from 1932. On the left is A3 2596 MANNA, which came out of Doncaster Works in February 1930 and went to Gateshead where it stayed until March 1943. It recalled the winner of the 1925 Derby. The engine had undoubtedly worked in from Newcastle. Next to it stands A3 2573 HARVESTER, named after the horse which was in a dead heat with St Gatien in the 1884 Derby. It was built by North British as an A1 and started work at Gateshead in October 1924. On conversion to an A3 in April 1928, the engine went to Haymarket with a corridor tender for working the non-stop 'Flying Scotsman', although it returned to Gateshead in July 1928. Then comes A1 2563 WILLIAM WHITELAW, named after the North British chairman and new to Haymarket from North British in August 1924. It also acquired a corridor tender in 1928 for the non-stop. Conversion to an A3 was in November 1942, following renaming TAGALIE in July 1941. On the right is Raven A2 Pacific 2402 CITY OF YORK, of North Eastern design but new to the LNER in March 1924. A Gateshead loco at the time, it has probably worked a secondary express from Newcastle. The engine was condemned in July 1936 while at based at York. 60085 MANNA was withdrawn from Gateshead in October 1964, 60074 HARVESTER from Neville Hill in April 1963 and 60064 TAGALIE from Grantham in September 1961.

with other sheds but within Haymarket itself, to have the cleanest, best maintained and most skilfully driven Pacific. These were the days of intimate associations between men and machines, such as Bill Nairn with 60004 WILLIAM WHITELAW, Bill Stevenson with 60027 MERLIN and Tommy Smith with 60031 GOLDEN PLOVER. Haymarket had a monopoly of Scottish A4s and the nickname 'Glamour Boys', which originated with RAF personnel, was certainly appropriate. When the regular manning system ceased, some engines were not quite as pristine as before, but every effort was made to keep the Pacifics on express passenger duties up to the former standard. Haymarket closed to steam in September 1963, but the prestige was still there in the form of eight Deltics which worked down the East Coast main line to Kings Cross for two decades. The InterCity HSTs which replaced them were based at Craigentinny. Haymarket continues to function as a maintenance and stabling point for diesel multiple units to this day.

Allocations at Haymarket (64B) 1950

A4 4-6-2: 60004 WILLIAM WHITELAW; 60009 UNION OF SOUTH AFRICA; 60011 EMPIRE OF INDIA; 60012 COMMONWEALTH OF AUSTRALIA; 60024 KINGFISHER; 60027 MERLIN; 60031 GOLDEN PLOVER

A3 4-6-2: 60035 WINDSOR LAD; 60037 HYPERION; 60041 SALMON TROUT; 60043 BROWN JACK; 60057 ORMONDE; 60087 BLENHEIM; 60090 GRAND PARADE; 60094 COLORADO; 60096 PAPYRUS; 60097 HUMORIST; 60098 SPION KOP; 60099 CALL BOY; 60100 SPEARMINT; 60101 CICERO

A1 4-6-2: 60152 HOLYROOD; 60159 BONNIE DUNDEE; 60160 AULD REEKIE; 60161 NORTH BRITISH; 60162 SAINT JOHNSTOUN

A2, A2/1, A2/3 4-6-2: 60507 HIGHLAND CHIEFTAIN; 60509 WAVERLEY; 60510 ROBERT THE BRUCE; 60519 HONEYWAY; 60529 PEARL DIVER; 60530 SAYAJIRAO; 60532 BLUE PETER; 60534 IRISH ELEGANCE; 60535 HORNET'S BEAUTY; 60536 TRIMBUSH

V2 2-6-2: 60816; 60834; 60882; 60927; 60951; 60959; 60972

B1 4-6-0: 61007 KLIPSPRINGER; 61076; 61081; 61178; 61221 SIR ALEXANDER ERSKINE-HILL; 61244 STRANG STEEL; 61245 MURRAY OF ELIBANK

D29 4-4-0: 62405 THE FAIR MAID

D30/2 4-4-0: 62437 ADAM WOODCOCK

D11/2 4-4-0: 62677 EDIE OCHILTREE; 62678 LUCKIE MUCKLEBACKIT; 62679 LORD GLENALLAN; 62683 HOBBIE ELLIOTT; 62685 MALCOLM GRAEME; 62690 THE LADY OF THE LAKE; 62691 LAIRD OF BALMAWHAPPLE; 62692 ALLAN-BANE; 62693 RODERICK DHU; 62694 JAMES FITZJAMES

D49/1 4-4-0: 62705 LANARKSHIRE; 62706 FORFARSHIRE; 62709 BERWICKSHIRE; 62719 PEEBLES-SHIRE; 62733 NORTHUMBERLAND

J36 0-6-0: 65240; 65243 MAUDE

V1/V3 2-6-2T: 67610; 67615; 67620

J88 0-6-0T: 68328; 68339

J83 0-6-0T: 68457; 68460; 68473; 68478; 68481

N15 0-6-2T: 69169; 69220

Peppercorn A1 60142 in magnificent repose at Haymarket, shortly after it was completed at Darlington Works in February 1949. This Gateshead engine had a regular working to Edinburgh on an early morning sleeping car express, then returned to Newcastle on the 10.00am 'Flying Scotsman'. Although originally wearing LNER apple green, it was repainted blue in October 1950 and named EDWARD FLETCHER at the same time, honouring the first Locomotive Superintendent of the North Eastern Railway, from 1854 to 1883. The Pacific was withdrawn from Gateshead in June 1965, having been absent for four years in the early 1960s at Heaton and Tweedmouth. Photograph John Robertson, The Transport Treasury.

Travelling Light

With Haymarket shed two miles west of Waverley along a busy main line, the numerous light engine movements which had to be slotted in between timetabled services were an inconvenient, albeit essential aspect of keeping the trains running. On 22 June 1959, Gateshead A1 60135 MADGE WILDFIRE in filthy condition backs down through Princes Street Gardens. It is probably on the way to Haymarket, but with the fire built up could be heading towards Corstorphine to collect empty coaching stock for the 3.43pm slow to Berwick. 60135, perpetuating the name of D29 2407 which was withdrawn in December 1947, went new to Gateshead in December 1948. From December 1960 to withdrawal in December 1962, the engine spent time at Copley Hill and Ardsley. Photograph The Transport Treasury.

A2 60537 BACHELORS BUTTON, in sparkling Haymarket condition, heads towards Mound Tunnel to join a train for the south at Waverley. Aberdeen had 60537 from July 1949, but considered single chimney A2s poor steamers and relegated them to secondary duties. During May 1951, the Grampian shed exchanged BACHELORS BUTTON for Haymarket's 60532 BLUE PETER, which had been fitted with a multiple valve regulator and double blastpipe in September 1949. Haymarket did not discriminate between the original and modified A2s. 60537 was transferred to St Margarets in November 1961, a year before withdrawal. Photograph The Transport Treasury.

On 25 June 1959, A3 60101 CICERO runs in reverse from Haymarket to Waverley for a Glasgow Queen Street or Aberdeen working. The Pacific was new to Haymarket in June 1930 as 2797, its name celebrating the winner of the 1905 Derby. From February 1937 to October 1940 the engine spent time at Dundee, Eastfield and St Margarets respectively, but then went back to Haymarket for a prolonged stay. It is seen here with the double chimney which was fitted in February 1959 and the new type LNER non-corridor tender that it had all its life. A move to St Margarets in January 1963 amounted to semi-retirement until withdrawal three months later.
Photograph
John Robertson, The Transport Treasury.

In clear afternoon air on 20 June 1959, 60011 EMPIRE OF INDIA returns to Haymarket shed from platform 11, still bearing the headboard revealing that it has made the non-stop run from Kings Cross on 'The Elizabethan'. The position of the nameboard meant that the true 'light engine' code, one headlamp centre bottom, could not be carried. This was one of the five A4s named after countries of the empire, specifically for working the pre-war non-stop 'Coronation'. Throughout its life, the engine ran with a corridor tender. New to Kings Cross shed as 4490 in June 1937, EMPIRE OF INDIA was transferred to Haymarket in March 1938 and remained there until June 1962. The double chimney was fitted in January 1958. For a couple of years prior to withdrawal in May 1964, 60011 was at Aberdeen for working the three-hour expresses to Glasgow Buchanan Street. Photograph John Robertson, The Transport Treasury.

Scotts and Glens

Some pre-grouping passenger classes continued in service despite a succession of newer engines which should have led to their demise. That was certainly the case with the North British Scotts and Glens, examples of which were still in evidence at Waverley as late as 1960. Together with their predecessors, these sturdy 4-4-0s were popular and reliable. Their early duties included express passenger work, which they inevitably lost in due course, but the stalwarts continued to haul long distance stopping trains right to the end. The first 4-4-0 in the country was introduced by Wheatley of the North British in 1871 and when the demand arose for locomotives capable of tackling the Waverley route with St Pancras-Edinburgh expresses, Drummond opted for the same wheel arrangement. They proved to be the first of a long line of classic North British 4-4-0s, of which the LNER inherited no less than 183. They comprised classes D25 to D36, which included rebuilt Drummond engines, various Holmes designs, Reid Intermediates and his first batch of Scotts. Reid's newest locos were superheated, the D30 Scotts and D34 Glens.

The initial build of 16 Scotts (LNER D29) appeared in 1909-11, principally for working non-stop expresses between Waverley and Carlisle. While two more were under construction at Cowlairs, Reid decided to try superheaters on them and the pair duly appeared in 1912 as a separate class which became LNER D30. They went to St Margarets and had a couple of years on non-stop passenger trains over the Waverley route before these were phased out. Another 25 were built from 1914 to 1920, the St Margarets and Haymarket engines being regularly employed on expresses to Carlisle, Glasgow and Perth. They had 6ft 6in driving wheels and always performed well on this work. It is hardly surprising that the influx of D11s, D49s, A1s, V2s and B1s had relegated them to far more mundane tasks by the 1950s, but they were still useful. The last two retired gracefully in June 1960, one of them from St Margarets.

A total of 32 Glens were built between 1913 and 1920. They were the final development of the North British 4-4-0, had 6ft 0in driving wheels and were, essentially, a superheated version of Reid's earlier Intermediates. The Glens proved efficient and versatile engines and were very popular with crews. Eastfield shed in Glasgow had a large proportion of the class for working the West Highland line, but as loads increased they had to be worked double headed. Nevertheless, they remained on that line despite the introduction of six-coupled classes. St Margarets had its share of Glens for passenger services to Berwick, Hawick, Dundee, Perth and Galashiels via Peebles, as well as fill-in turns on the Edinburgh suburban network. The D34s also worked express goods trains to Perth and Newcastle. The last two were withdrawn in 1961, although GLEN DOUGLAS in North British livery continued to work specials for another year and is now preserved.

A batch of fifteen North British class J 4-4-0s were built at Cowlairs Works in 1914 and 412 LAIRD O' MONKBARNS was one of the first, entering traffic in April of that year. It was named after the provost of Fairport, widely thought to be Arbroath, in Scott's novel *The Antiquary*, set during the Jacobite revolution. For some time it was at Carlisle Canal and regularly worked St Pancras trains forward to Edinburgh over the Waverley route. As D30 9412, the engine spent some of its LNER career at Haymarket, then moved to St Margarets where it spent the whole of the 1950s, renumbered 62421. Seen here below St Andrews House on 18 March 1950, LAIRD O' MONKBARNS received a new boiler just over a year later, which no doubt helped it to become one of the last two survivors. Withdrawal from St Margarets came in June 1960. Photograph John Robertson, The Transport Treasury.

D30/2 62437 ADAM WOODCOCK leaves Waverley with the 12.05pm to Dunbar on 10 April 1952. Built at Cowlairs, North British 428 went into express passenger service at Haymarket during August 1915. The LNER altered the appearance of the 'Scott', then 9428, by removing the characteristic NB smokebox wingplates in the early 1920s and replacing the Westinghouse brakes with steam brakes during the mid-1930s. Main line work was largely confined to piloting expresses by this time. Withdrawal of 62437 from decidedly pedestrian duties came in June 1958. The author has failed to discover where Adam Woodcock appeared in Scott's novels! Photograph John Robertson, The Transport Treasury.

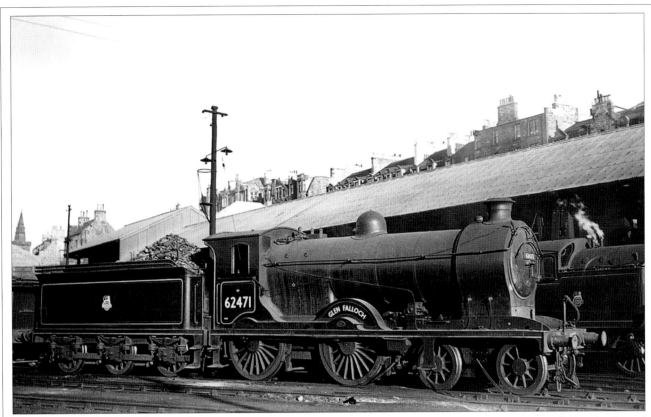

D34 62471 GLEN FALLOCH basks in evening sunshine at St Margarets on 28 July 1951, with the coaling bank and tenements of London Road forming a backdrop. This was one of the first batch of five, which were completed at Cowlairs in the autumn of 1913. In typical North British fashion, they took up spare numbers 149, 221, 256, 258 and 266. GLEN FALLOCH, named after the pass which took the West Highland line from the head of Loch Lomond to Crianlarich, was new as 266 in October 1913. It was a long term resident of St Margarets and one of those equipped to carry a small snowplough. On most D34s so fitted, this was for the West Highland line, but in this case it proved useful for the Peebles - Galashiels section. 62471 was withdrawn from St Margarets in March 1960. Photograph John Robertson, The Transport Treasury.

The final batch of twelve D34s came out of Cowlairs in 1920, the first being 504 GLEN ALADALE. It was new in April and carried the name of an extremely remote valley bordering Loch Shiel about seven miles from Glenfinnan on the West Highland Extension. As 9504, it was at St Margarets during LNER days and had its share of fast passenger work, filling-in turns on suburban duties and express goods trains to Perth and Newcastle. The engine, by then 62488, is seen at St Margarets on 28 August 1951 against the familiar coaling stage and London Road tenements. After nationalisation, this D34 spent a fair amount of time at Hawick on local passenger work and occasionally appeared at Carlisle, a place not previously associated with Glens. GLEN ALADALE was withdrawn in October 1960. Photograph John Robertson, The Transport Treasury.

On a glorious sunny evening, probably during the summer of 1951, D11/2 62691 LAIRD OF BALMAWHAPPLE barks out of Haymarket with a stopping train bound for Fife via the Forth Bridge. The engine, built by Armstrong Whitworth as 6398, went new to Eastfield in November 1924 where it was one of the spares to cover No.1 link between Glasgow and Edinburgh. It also worked specials. In December 1931 it moved to St Margarets and had regular outings to Perth, Dundee, Carlisle and Glasgow, mainly on secondary passenger duties. A move to Haymarket in April 1943 saw the engine on similar workings, portrayed beautifully in this view, but their Directors were never kept as clean as the Pacifics. With little to occupy its time, 62691 languished at Polmont for a while before withdrawal in November 1961. The Laird was a somewhat violent, unsavoury character in Scott's first novel *Waverley*. Photograph John Robertson, The Transport Treasury.

Back at its old home, D11/2 62674 FLORA MACIVOR rests at Haymarket shed in January 1952. The loco has been turned and coaled and is in full steam, probably for working an afternoon stopping train to Glasgow via Falkirk or Bathgate. After completion by Kitson in August 1924, the erstwhile 6381 went to Haymarket for top link service between Waverley and Queen Street. It migrated to Eastfield in August 1943 and continued to serve Central Scotland for a decade and a half, though rarely taxed to its full ability. After a period in store at Thornton, 62674 was condemned in July 1961. The original Flora, from *Waverley*, was a beautiful, passionate clan heroine during the Jacobite rebellion of 1745. Photograph John Robertson, The Transport Treasury.

Directors

Immediately after Grouping, Gresley was mainly concerned with developing Pacifics for the East Coast main line, but there was a pressing need for new engines of lesser dimensions in some sections, including the North British. Therefore, the LNER decided to build additional locos based on certain existing classes. Robinson's 'Improved Directors' of 1919-22 were largely regarded as his finest design for express passenger work on the Great Central and a further 24 were ordered at the end of 1923 for Scotland. They were delivered from Kitson of Leeds and Armstrong Whitworth of Newcastle upon Tyne during 1924 and carried somewhat whimsical names from the novels of Sir Walter Scott, continuing a North British tradition. Although they had alien characteristics such as right hand drive, different firing arrangements and a tendency to be sluggish starters, it seems that most Scottish crews warmed to them.

Classified D11/2, several Scottish Directors went new to Haymarket and Eastfield for Edinburgh-Glasgow services over the main line. Each was assigned regular sets of men and the usual shift pattern was to work an express in one direction and a stopping train on the return leg. Other duties included the 'Queen of Scots' Pullman and the more important trains via Bathgate and Airdrie. Occasionally a Director piloted a Pacific on heavy trains to Newcastle. The St Margarets allocation worked mainly to Perth, although Dundee and eventually Glasgow and Carlisle featured in their rosters. After a mere four or five years, the Haymarket Directors lost some of the best Edinburgh - Glasgow jobs to D49s. Increasingly, they were used on slower trains to Dundee, the Fife Coast, Falkirk and Stirling, the arrival of B1s in the late 1940s making them more or less superfluous. St Margarets D11s had less to lose, although these engines also gravitated to mundane duties on all routes out of Waverley as well. During the late 1950s, the Directors spent a lot of time in store and were only steamed when peak traffic required their services.

Volcanic crags and threads of steel frame St Margarets D11/2 6391 WIZARD OF THE MOOR at the east end of Waverley in 1935. In later years, this Armstrong Whitworth engine was something of a nomad. It went new to St Margarets in October 1924 and enjoyed quite a few years of fast work, notably to Perth, but transfer to Haymarket in April 1943 saw it on slower jobs. Then came residence at Eastfield from September 1945 on similar secondary workings, including journeys to Waverley. In April 1957, then renumbered 62684, the loco looked like having a change of career when it went to St Rollox for Glasgow Buchanan Street - Fife services. After a few days the authorities had second thoughts and WIZARD OF THE MOOR returned to Eastfield where it remained until its demise in October 1959. The wizard was the deformed recluse of bleak Mucklestone Moor in *The Black Dwarf*. Photograph H.N. Shepherd, The Transport Treasury.

Above. On 3 July 1954, a Fife service has unloaded at platform 20 and D49/1 62713 ABERDEEN-SHIRE of Thornton shed departs for Craigentinny carriage sidings with the empty stock. It is 1.30pm on this hot summer day and all the coach windows are dropped. Delivered from Darlington as 249 in February 1928, the loco spent its time at Dundee until the early 1950s, principally for working Aberdeen trains. Note the rebuilt Great Central tender. 62713 was withdrawn in September 1957, only the second of the class to go. Photograph John Robertson, The Transport Treasury.

Below. One of Haymarket's Shires, D49/1 62709 BERWICKSHIRE, leaves South Calton Tunnel and ambles into Waverley with a stopping train from Hawick on 10 April 1952. Gresley corridor stock has been provided for this Waverley route local. The engine, seen here with an unrebuilt Great Central tender, began life during January 1928 as 277. It was not a Haymarket engine until the end of the LNER era, although the loco spent whole of the 1950s there until withdrawal in January 1960. When new, St Margarets D49s would have been seen on trains like this, but they also worked heavy expresses between Edinburgh and Carlisle with no difficulty. Photograph John Robertson, The Transport Treasury.

Shires

Platform 17 at Waverley, probably during 1947, and D49/1 2712 MORAYSHIRE is ready to leave with a stopping train for Dundee or Perth. This engine was rather a wanderer, starting at Dundee shed in 1928 as 246, then moving to Perth during 1931. It was at St Margarets in 1950, Thornton in 1959 and Hawick in 1961. Before it was built, the intention was to apply the name FIFESHIRE to 246, but strangely this county was never honoured by a name on a D49, despite the LNER monopoly there. As the last of the class to be withdrawn, in July 1961, 62712 was saved for preservation. Photograph The Transport Treasury.

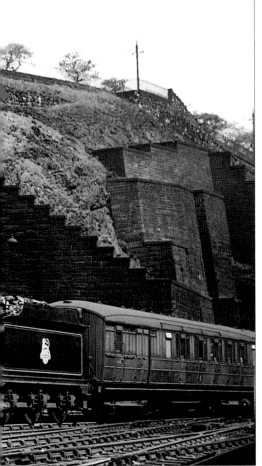

Once he was satisfied that the A1 Pacifics would meet requirements for express passenger work, Gresley turned his attention to locomotives for other fast passenger duties. There was certainly a need, as many North British and North Eastern engines were due for early withdrawal. The result was a substantial class of 3-cylinder 4-4-0s with 6ft 8in driving wheels, the first new LNER passenger design and the last of this wheel arrangement produced by the company. A total of 76 D49s emerged from Darlington Works between 1927 and 1935. Part of the remit was that the engines had to be powerful enough to replace North British Atlantics on Carlisle and Aberdeen expresses. Of the first batch of 36, nearly two-thirds went to Scotland, including two to Haymarket and six to St Margarets. They all carried the names of counties and, appropriately, the Scottish ones were named after shires north of the border. Unfortunately, they tended to be somewhat rough riders and were not liked that much by crews.

Initially, Haymarket's allocation ousted D11s from Glasgow services, but they did eventually replace Atlantics on Dundee and Newcastle workings. By 1943, the shed had twelve of them. In turn, the D49s were gradually displaced from the best Glasgow jobs by Pacifics. St Margarets engines basically took over duties previously done by Atlantics and they put in some very good performances on expresses and stopping trains over the Waverley route. They also had fast workings to Glasgow, Perth and Dundee, hauled express goods to Newcastle and enjoyed rather more pedestrian trips to Peebles and Galashiels. Denied a dedicated allocation of Pacifics, St Margarets still used D49s on its Glasgow turns until a batch of V2s arrived. After this, they were employed on all manner of duties, including stopping trains to Carlisle. The advent of B1s during the late 1940s more or less finished off fast work for the 4-4-0s and several of the class gravitated to Thornton where they were employed on slow trains to Edinburgh prior to their demise.

K3 61900 leaves Mound Tunnel with a Saturday extra from Waverley to Dundee Tay Bridge on 20 June 1959. This train was something of a scratch set, the first two coaches being of LMS and LNER origin respectively. The engine was one of a batch of twenty built by Armstrong Whitworth of Newcastle and went new to Gateshead shed as 1101 in March 1931. Within days of being delivered, it made a little bit of railway history. Along with sisters 1100 and 1102, it hauled one of three Newcastle-Kings Cross Cup Final specials, followed a week later by a heavy York-London excursion. Such lengthy passenger workings were, it is believed, never repeated by a K3. After a short spell at March shed, 1101 went to St Margarets in 1941 and played its part in moving the vital and tremendously heavy wartime goods traffic. 61900 ended its days at St Margarets in March 1960. In this view it seems to have a home-made 64A shedplate with the figures widely spaced. Photograph John Robertson, The Transport Treasury.

The prototype K4 was 3441, which was named LOCH LONG, thus perpetuating the 1933-34 scheme whereby thirteen K2s regularly employed on West Highland trains were named after lochs near the line. Gresley's new K4 entered service at Eastfield shed in January 1937 and soon proved a very sound design, hauling 300 tons over the Fort William route as opposed to the limit of 190 tons for a Glen. Later that year, the engine did a round trip of 244 miles from Glasgow Queen Street to Fort William and back, a feat which had been almost unknown until then. As a result of these achievements, five more K4s were ordered early in 1938. In BR lined black, 61993 LOCH LONG heads through Princes Street Gardens on 20 June 1959 with a stopping train for Thornton Junction, formed of non-corridors. The loco had recently been transferred to Thornton shed and remained there until condemned in October 1961. Photograph John Robertson, The Transport Treasury.

Moguls

During 1917 Gresley decided that a new express goods loco was required, based on the existing Great Northern 2-cylinder 2-6-0s which became LNER class K2. The concept materialised in 1920 as a 3-cylinder 2-6-0 with an unprecedented 6ft 0in diameter boiler. Ten engines were built for the GN and they were classified K3 by the LNER, which embraced them as a standard design. Between 1924 and 1937 another 183 were built by the company at Doncaster and Darlington, as well as by private firms Armstrong Whitworth, Robert Stephenson and North British. Production came to an end with the development of the V2 2-6-2. St Margarets found the K3s ideal for fast goods workings, especially those from Edinburgh to Newcastle, and had five of them in 1937, the total growing to no less than 24 by 1949. Although not primarily passenger engines, these LNER 2-6-0s

were seen on Waverley - Perth trains fairly frequently and occasionally ventured to Glasgow and Carlisle on expresses. They also proved useful on specials and summer Saturday extras. The K3s were versatile and Edinburgh crews liked them a lot.

In complete contrast, the K4s were very specialised machines. The West Highland line from Craigendoran to Fort William began and ended virtually on the shore, but in between there were ferocious gradients and severe curves through the mountains to reach Currour summit, 1,347ft above sea level. To make matters worse, the nature of certain bridges meant that axle loads were restricted. Prior to grouping, Glens were used from Glasgow to Fort William, but with the advent of heavier trains double-heading became necessary. Although K2s proved satisfactory, Gresley decided to design 2-6-0s specifically for

the route. The six K4s were built at Darlington in 1937-38 and featured an ample K2 boiler, cylinders of the size fitted to K3s and unusually small 5ft 2in driving wheels. In essence, they were powerful yet lightweight locomotives which took stiff climbs and snaking track in their stride. Nine coach trains, including a heavy restaurant car, were no problem. Unfortunately, they were not suited to fast running and parts of the motion frequently worked loose on the level section between Craigendoran and Glasgow Queen Street. From the early 1950s, the K4s were largely confined to goods traffic, including trips to Edinburgh. Apart from one which had been rebuilt as a 2-cylinder K1 in 1945, they gravitated to Thornton shed in 1959 and continued to visit the capital, mainly on goods.

Obviously there was a lot of extra traffic on Saturday 20 June 1959, as all manner of engines were pressed into passenger service, including at least two of Thornton's K4s, which the shed regarded as freight locos. In bright afternoon sunshine, 61994 THE GREAT MARQUESS eases a train from Thornton Junction through Princes Street Gardens towards Mound Tunnel and Waverley. Darlington Works turned out the five production K4s during 1938, and they were all named after Scottish clan chiefs associated with the mountainous country around the West Highland line. THE GREAT MARQUESS went to Eastfield in July 1938 as 3442, although it was actually named MACCAILEIN MÓR for a few days. In 1941 the engine demonstrated its power by arriving at Waverley with a 13-coach Glasgow-Leeds train. When withdrawn from Thornton in December 1961, 61994 was purchased for preservation and reverted to 3442 in apple green livery. Photograph John Robertson, The Transport Treasury.

On the bright summer afternoon of 17 July 1953, the North British Hotel clock shows that there is a quarter of an hour to go before V2 60825 is due to leave with the 2.30pm Saturdays only from Waverley to Dundee. Completed by Darlington Works in January 1938, 4796 moved from Doncaster to St Margarets in October 1945 and was there when withdrawn in April 1964. The V2s were such useful engines that other sheds often commandeered them. For instance, a month after this photograph was taken 60825 was employed on a Perth-Glasgow Buchanan Street passenger train. Photograph John Robertson, The Transport Treasury.

By 25 January 1965 there was plenty of interest in travelling behind the thinning ranks of steam locomotives and Dundee V2 60919 receives undivided attention from the first coach on that day. It is leaving Waverley on a train for its home town, overshadowed by the National Gallery of Scotland which had recently been deprived of 120 years of grime from the railway. 60919 was still very active in April 1966 when it was observed in Edinburgh having hauled the Dundee-Blackpool as far as the capital. New as 4890 in September 1941, and an Aberdeen Ferryhill engine for a long time, it was finally withdrawn in September 1966. Photograph J.A.M. Vaughan, The Transport Treasury.

V2s

With the increased weight and speed of goods trains, Gresley decided that a more powerful mixed traffic locomotive was required. The 2-6-2 configuration, featuring trailing wheels, permitted a wide firebox which enabled more steam to be produced. This was a logical development of the K3 2-6-0. Although the original drawing showed a smaller version of the P2 2-8-2, the eventual design was more conventional and incorporated a shortened A3 boiler, three cylinders and 6ft 2in driving wheels. The first five V2s emerged from Doncaster Works in 1936 and were an instant success. In fact, the new 2-6-2s soon proved they were a perfectly good substitute for a Pacific on express passenger trains. They were allowed the same load as an A3 or A4 in Scotland. Eventually, a total of 184 were turned out by Doncaster and Darlington, the last one appearing in 1944.

As early as 1936, Dundee V2s were working to Edinburgh on passenger, fish and goods trains. Then in 1939 two examples went to St Margarets and were employed on passenger services to Glasgow as well as fast goods over the East Coast main line. By 1940 the allocation was up to six. Haymarket received one in 1941 and a couple more in 1943, these sharing passenger work with Pacifics. In Scotland as elsewhere, there was an enormous amount of heavy goods work for the V2s during World War Two and it has been stated that these were the engines that won the war. In 1947 St Margarets had none on its books, yet Haymarket was home to fourteen. Gradually, the situation reversed to the extent that in 1961 Haymarket had none, but St Margarets had accumulated 28. During the 1950s, Edinburgh V2s proved very useful on holiday traffic and sometimes ventured as far south as York with extras. The St Margarets engines enjoyed a fitting finale as they had plenty of work because of the unreliability of diesels. In April 1966, 60868 even worked the 'Aberdonian' sleeper from Edinburgh to Aberdeen. The very last V2 in service, 60836, still graced Waverley a matter of days prior to being withdrawn from Dundee at the end of December 1966.

Despite the brave new world of diesel traction, a Swindon Inter-City set is creating more smoke than 60888 on this sunny afternoon, possibly during the winter of 1961. The V2 is on an Aberdeen express and had been at Ferryhill since moving north from Gateshead in October 1945. From 1949 and throughout the 1950s, Aberdeen V2s were often employed on passenger and fast goods workings over the former Caledonian route through Perth to Glasgow Buchanan Street. 60888 was withdrawn from Ferryhill in December 1962, having started life as 4859 in December 1939. Photograph P. Wilson, G.R. Whitelaw Collection.

No less than 290 B1s were built by the North British Locomotive Co. at Queens Park Works, Glasgow. They included a batch of 150 which emerged between May 1947 and September 1948, a rate of one every 3¼ working days! One of the first was 1197, which went new to Eastfield. It is seen here at Waverley's platform 14 a few weeks after delivery, in charge of a stopping service to Glasgow Queen Street. The crew would have been pleased to get this engine rather than a D11. Livery is Apple Green and equipment for the electric headlights is in place, although the lamps have not been fitted. Standing at platform 13 and overlooked by elegant Victorian additions to the Old Town is 1116, a slightly earlier North British product. Photograph John Robertson, The Transport Treasury.

On 7 October 1950, a bright clear day in Edinburgh, 61178 takes the Forth Bridge lines with an early afternoon local service to Crail on the Fife Coast, invariably a Haymarket B1 turn. This engine, which entered service in June 1947, was one of fifty built by Vulcan Foundry of Newton-le-Willows, Lancashire. Clearly a shed favourite at the time, 61178 gained a reputation for being turned out in gleaming external condition by the men who regularly worked it. In an appropriate setting, the trees are taking on an autumn hue and the National Gallery looks as magnificent as ever. Photograph John Robertson, The Transport Treasury.

B1s

Edward Thompson's large class of mixed traffic 4-6-0s was probably the best example of his standardisation policy. Conceived at the height of World War 2, they were designed to replace some of the motley collection of 4-6-0s, 4-4-2s, 4-4-0s, 2-6-0s and even 0-6-0s inherited from pre-grouping companies or actually built by the LNER. This was a broad remit and involved a very wide range of duties. By and large, they achieved this aim, but intended victims such as D30s, D34s and D11s continued to find employment in the Edinburgh area, as already noted. The first drawings appeared in 1941 and, after several modifications, detailed work began in 1942. A batch of ten were ordered in July of that year, 8301 SPRINGBOK being the first to enter service the following December. After a lengthy gestation period involving much trial running, the last of the initial build was completed in June 1944. With the engines proving a success, thirty more had already been ordered the previous month and the intention to build a further 370 was announced in 1945. They were turned out by Darlington Works, Gorton Works, Vulcan Foundry and North

British Loco between April 1946 and April 1952, the Glasgow firm winning the lion's share of orders. Apart from an accident victim in 1950, the B1s were withdrawn between the end of 1961 and autumn 1967.

Shortly after emerging from Darlington Works in 1943, 8303 IMPALA went to Haymarket for trials between Waverley and Glasgow, Perth, Dundee and Carlisle. It proved a free-steaming machine with very good attributes such as rapid acceleration and the ability to pull away easily from stations on gradients. In fact, Thompson's 4-6-0s were ideal for semi-fast workings over Scotland's hilly main lines. Edinburgh was an early beneficiary, Haymarket having eight B1s by the end of 1947. There were nine at St Margarets in 1952 and the shed had amassed no less than 24 by 1961. Haymarket engines were used on passenger services to Glasgow, Perth and Dundee, together with slow trains to Carlisle. The depot also ran in some brand new locos for a few days after they emerged from North British. Besides a share of passenger work over all the main lines, St Margarets B1s worked certain fast goods trains to

Carlisle and Newcastle. Both sheds also used them on local jobs to Corstorphine and over the Suburban line. Eastfield, Dundee and Carlisle engines worked regularly into Waverley as well.

Of the 410 B1s, only ten were built by the former Great Central workshops at Gorton in Manchester and all were based in Scotland. One of them, **61340**, is seen in Princes Street Gardens on 15 August 1959 waiting to back on to a morning Glasgow train. The Eastfield engine, new there in November 1948, has a complete set of electric lighting and the angular dome cover is characteristic of the Gorton batch. V3 67620, on a local to Dunfermline, was one of the great survivors of the class. It entered service at Haymarket as V1 2920 in October 1931 and was finally withdrawn from Gateshead in November 1964, many months after numerous B1s less than half its age. **Photograph John Robertson, The Transport Treasury.**

The pristine condition of Haymarket Pacifics was legendary, but St Margarets V tanks were also kept very smart and with regularly rostered drivers, some of them were immaculate. During the early 1950s, 67629 in the care of Driver A Brand was acknowledged as the star. With burnished fittings, the V1 arrives at Waverley with a service from North Berwick on 10 April 1952. Earlier, it had been outstationed at North Berwick, a sub-shed renowned for turning out clean engines, especially on 'The Lothian Coast Express'. 67629 began life as 2929 in February 1935 and was allocated to St Margarets where it remained until withdrawn in May 1962. It was never converted into a V3. Note the plain bunker, as opposed to the hopper on 67668 and coal rail type on 2906 and 7610. Photograph John Robertson, The Transport Treasury.

Seen here at the east end of Waverley in 1935, V1 2906, one of the first batch, entered service at St Margarets in December 1930. Day to day workings included Musselburgh, Corstorphine, Gorebridge, Rosewell, Bonnyrigg, Galashiels and Peebles, as well as trips over the South Suburban line and visits to Leith Central. As 67606, the engine was converted to a V3 in December 1952. From 1956 to 1959 it had something of a rural retreat, allocated to Hawick for working the Kelso branch from St Boswells sub-shed. Withdrawal from St Margarets came in December 1962. Photograph The Transport Treasury.

Local Passenger

For over three decades, the vast roofed area at the east end of Waverley has been under used by passenger trains to say the least, no doubt prompting some people to wonder why it was ever provided. A century ago, just after the station was rebuilt, the situation was very different. At that time an abundance of suburban, local and main line stopping services headed east past Calton Hill to all manner of destinations near and far. The peak years were 1903 to 1925, between the last new line opening and the first withdrawals. During those two decades there were seventeen different services, some admittedly rather sparse and others reduced in frequency towards the end of the period. Places served were very varied, from prim suburbs to streets of dockside warehouses and mill towns in valleys to hamlets in the hills. There were some local services from the west end of Waverley, but apart from those to South Queensferry and Corstorphine, they were largely stopping trains on the main lines.

In the east, it started with the North British main line and stations such as Portobello and Prestonpans, together with a branch to the county town of Haddington. Then came the first part of the Waverley route, beginning with a branch to Gorebridge in the coalfield and the extension to Hawick. Musselburgh by the sea and Dalkeith a few miles inland acquired steam-hauled services, having previously been served by horse-drawn carriages on the pioneering Edinburgh & Dalkeith Railway. A branch opened to the important coastal town of North Berwick, followed by the straggling upland line to Peebles which served the coalfield villages of Bonnyrigg and Rosewell. The nearby settlement of Polton then gained its own branch. Granton, North Leith and their respective docks, originally reached from Canal Street terminus at right

A dull and murky early afternoon scene at the east end of Waverley on 10 April 1952. Nevertheless, the North British Hotel, Governor's House and Scottish Office still maintain a domineering presence as V1 67668 departs with a stopping train to Dunbar or North Berwick. The engine was one of fifteen in the 1936 building programme destined for the Great Eastern section and as 448 entered service at Stratford during October 1938. Displaced by the influx of new L1 2-6-4Ts, it went to St Margarets in 1949. A high pressure boiler was fitted in 1951, but the upgrade to V3 did not materialise until May 1954. Withdrawal from St Margarets came in December 1962. Photograph John Robertson, The Transport Treasury.

angles to Waverley, benefited from services to the main station after the opening of a new connection. Remote Macmerry in the eastern part of the coalfield, Penicuik in the Esk Valley and Roslin, Loanhead and Glencorse in the southern coalfield were the next places to have passenger trains. The South Side loop served, and even stimulated the growing suburbs. Gullane on the coast and Gifford on the edge of the Lammermuir Hills eventually joined the route map. Finally, the large terminus at Leith Central opened.

A range of North British classes worked this assortment of lines while the company was independent, although new 4-4-2Ts and fairly new 0-4-4Ts, LNER C16 and G9 respectively, handled many suburban and important medium distance local services by the grouping of 1923. Downgraded express passenger engines played their part and there were some interesting survivors from an earlier era, notably the quaint yet competent D51 4-4-0Ts on the Gifford branch. The LNER introduced Sentinel steam railcars and brought in engines from other areas, such as Great Eastern F4 2-4-2Ts and Great Northern N2 0-6-2Ts. However, the most significant

Local services from the east end of Waverley.
Route, together with duration of service.
Dunbar/Berwick 1846 - Present
Haddington 1846 - 1949
Gorebridge/Hawick 1847/49 - 1969
Dalkeith 1847 - 1942
Musselburgh 1847 - 1964
North Berwick 1850 - Present
Peebles 1855 - 1962
Polton 1867 - 1951
Granton 1868 - 1925 *
North Leith 1868 - 1947 *
Macmerry 1872 - 1925
Penicuik 1872 - 1951
Roslin/Glencorse 1874/77 - 1933
South Side Suburban 1884 - 1962
Gullane 1898 - 1932
Gifford 1901 - 1933
Leith Central 1903 - 1952
***** Served from Canal Street between 1847 and 1868.

development was in December 1928 when Gresley was authorised to provide new 2-6-2Ts for central Scotland. Altogether, 92 engines of this type were constructed at Doncaster between September 1930 and April 1940. At first they had 180lb sq in boilers and were classified V1, but in January 1939 it was decided to increase the pressure to 200lb sq in and the last ten duly emerged in this form as V3s. Many V1s were

subsequently rebuilt to V3s. Although Gresley's 2-6-2Ts also worked on the Great Eastern section and in northern England, they became synonymous with local services over former North British lines around Glasgow and Edinburgh. St Margarets had a dozen or more for many years and they found their way on to most lines around the city. The last of the class was withdrawn in November 1964.

Waverley Bridge and the lower reaches of the Old Town rise above V1 7610 as it prepares to back on to a Fife or Larbert train in the summer of 1947. This engine was among the initial build of 28 and went new to Haymarket in April 1931 as 2910. Other duties involved the Corstorphine, Gorebridge and South Suburban services, as well as Glasgow Queen Street Low Level and Hyndland via Airdrie. Never reboilered as a V3, 67610 was condemned at Haymarket in June 1961. Some of these V tanks gave remarkable service, notably 67614 which accumulated nearly a million miles, mainly in the Glasgow area. Photograph W Hermiston, The Transport Treasury.

The Pilot

During the 1950s, five J83 0-6-0Ts were maintained in immaculate black livery by St Margarets and Haymarket for station pilot duties at Waverley. In May 1953, East End Pilot 68474 simmers between duties in one of the loco byes near Waverley East cabin. The dour concrete box, erected during the resignalling of 1936-38, can be seen in the left background. In front of it is one of the ornate gantries dating from the reconstruction of Waverley in 1892-1900, now carrying colour light signals. Keeping 68474 company is an ancient wooden-bodied wagon still lettered 'The Gas Light Coke Co.' On the right, newer wagons stand in the sidings at Waverley Goods depot and a Union Jack flutters above them, this being Coronation year. Even here, there is a reminder of Edinburgh's volcanic past in the form of distant Salisbury Crags on the flank of Arthur's Seat. Photograph John Robertson, The Transport Treasury.

The North British class D 0-6-0Ts, later LNER J83, came about because of an increase of traffic as a result of the Boer War coinciding with a shortage of engines for shunting and short distance goods work. Holmes designed them and twenty were built by Neilson Reid, the same number by Sharp Stewart. They were dispersed throughout the North British system and most sheds had at least one of them. With St Andrews House in the background, 68474 stands in an engine siding at the east end of Waverley on 14 April 1951. Uniquely, it still carries the apple green livery and LNER lettering applied in 1946, despite the BR number. The engine was completed by Sharp Stewart during April 1901 and entered service as North British 827, becoming LNER 9827 and eventually 8474. In this view, the tallow cup for lubricating the inside cylinders can clearly be seen on the smokebox. Photograph John Robertson, The Transport Treasury.

It is 21 May 1955 and 68474 looks just as smart as it did in the photograph taken two years earlier. Dominated by a particularly harsh corner of Calton Hill, the J83 prepares to manoeuvre main line stock into the east end of Waverley, a Gresley brake in red and cream being nearest the engine. Of necessity, the crew are very vigilant as even a minor derailment would cause havoc with the working of the station. Other members of the class did not have such a high profile, but certainly put in some work. For instance, 68477 had covered over two million miles when it retired from St Margarets in December 1962 and 68464 had spent the whole of its 57 year existence on Leith Walk pilot duties prior to withdrawal from the same shed in March 1958. For a while in the early 1940s, one very high profile job for a J83 was an early morning suburban passenger train from Corstorphine to Waverley, loading up to twelve coaches. Apparently, there were some spirited performances on this duty! Waverley East End Pilot 68474 was withdrawn in April 1958. Photograph P Wilson, G R Whitelaw Collection.

Pilot engines for the west end of Waverley were worked by Haymarket men from what amounted to a sub-shed at that end of the station. Some time around 1957, J83 68481 draws empty coaching stock through Princes Street Gardens. From this angle, several points of interest can be seen. The shunter's step below the bunker is prominent and there is a former loco destination board wedged at the back to add a little more coal capacity. Note the square safety valve casing, indicating that this was one of the J83s fitted with a new boiler in 1951. This view also proves that the top of the boiler was kept as clean as the rest of the engine! Although a long term resident of Haymarket, indeed one of the pilots painted in LNER green, this particular loco spent some of its early years banking passenger trains up Cowlairs Incline out of Glasgow Queen Street. It was withdrawn in February 1962, one of the last ten to go. Photograph P. Wilson, G.R. Whitelaw Collection.

Unsung Heroes

St Margarets shed was a curious place, with a history characterised by anomalies. It had one of the largest allocations in Britain, yet it occupied an awkward, cramped and potentially dangerous site. It was the senior depot in the group (latterly 64A), but for decades lost out to Haymarket when it came to 'glamour' turns on expresses. Despite its preponderance of humdrum duties, St Margarets outlasted the more prestigious outfit on the other side of Edinburgh as far as steam was concerned, and even acquired numerous Pacifics towards the end, as seen earlier. Yet 64A has now vanished, virtually without trace, whereas Haymarket survives as a stabling and servicing point.

For the opening of the North British Railway from Berwick in 1846, an engine shed was provided two miles east of North Bridge in an area known as Jock's Lodge. It occupied a narrow wedge between the tracks and the Great North Road, which crossed the line at an acute angle. Until the Edinburgh & Glasgow Railway was acquired in 1865 and Cowlairs Works developed, engines, coaches and wagons were built here as well. With traffic increasing and new lines opening, the original 16-road roundhouse became overwhelmed, so a carriage shed on the opposite side of the main line was demolished and

replaced by a 6-road straight shed for locomotives in the late 1860s. Facilities for North Eastern engines were also built, a sad reflection of the dark days of the North British when it could not be trusted to take over East Coast expresses with any degree of reliability. By the early 1900s, St Margarets appeared to be under siege. The shed was home to over 200 engines and the main road a matter of yards away was lined with tenements which soared above the tracks. Even worse, the split site proved lethal for some employees attempting to cross the main line, which was on a reverse curve obscured at its west end by the road bridge.

Despite years of uneasiness over motive power between the North Eastern and North British, the latter did go on to produce some fine engines. These included the Reid Atlantics, some of which were allocated to St Margarets for express duties. It was clearly a blow when Haymarket was favoured as the principal shed for express passenger work. Admittedly, the large LNER Pacifics seemed more at home in the spacious meadows of Merchiston rather than the tight confines of Jock's Lodge. St Margarets managed to retain some main line passenger duties, notably those over the Waverley route, which were handled by D11s and D49s, even A1s

and A3s for a while, then B1s and V2s. During early BR days, there were ex-North British 4-4-0s for lighter passenger work and tanks for suburban services. However, the dominant role for this east end shed was the movement of goods and minerals, everything from express freight to dock shunting. There were 2-6-0s, an army of 0-6-0s in various guises and the little 0-4-0ST 'Pugs'. Some these Y9s were certainly loyal. When 68095 was withdrawn in December 1962, it had spent all of its 75 years since emerging from Cowlairs Works in 1887 allocated to St Margarets, mainly plodding around Leith Docks.

The only way St Margarets could cope with its huge allocation of up to 220 locomotives was to keep some of them at various sub-sheds and other stabling points. The former were at Dolphinton, Dunbar, Galashiels, Gifford, Gullane, Lauder, Longniddry, Musselburgh, North Berwick, Peebles, Penicuik, Polton, Roslin, Seafield and Selkirk. In addition, there were 'signing-on points', where engines were continuously at work and crews reported for duty, at Craigentinny, Duddingston, Granton, Hardengreen, Heriothill, Leith Walk, Niddrie, North Leith, Portobello and South Leith. Even so, it was still impossible to accommodate the remaining locos at

The final development of a long line of North British 0-6-0s was the superheated version of Reid class B, later LNER J37. A total of 104 were built between 1914 and 1921, St Margarets having up to 26 of them from the 1920s to the 1950s. With their high-pitched boilers, they had a powerful appearance which was certainly not deceptive. When new, some of them had to cope with heavy wartime traffic and crews were always proud of their J37s. Even after larger engines appeared, they continued to work express goods trains on the main lines out of Edinburgh and frequently appeared on local passenger services. In evening light on 5 May 1951, 64555 complements the tenements overlooking St Margarets shed. As 437, it was new from Cowlairs Works in June 1916 and lasted until October 1964. Photograph John Robertson, The Transport Treasury.

St Margarets on Sunday after they were serviced. Instead, some were sent to Portobello where they stood on a running loop alongside the main line, simmering ready for work on Monday morning. They were the days of plenty, but after a period providing refuge for, among other engines, some of Haymarket's now scruffy Pacifics, St Margarets closed in April 1967 and most of the site has since been redeveloped.

Allocations at St Margarets (64A) 1950
5MT 4-6-0: 45036; 45085
2MT 2-6-0: 46460; 46461; 46462
2F 0-6-0T: 47162
V2 2-6-2: 60825; 60836; 60848; 60894; 60980
B1 4-6-0: 61002 IMPALA; 61061; 61067; 61242 ALEXANDER REITH GRAY; 61277; 61341; 61354; 61355; 61356; 61357; 61358; 61359
K3 2-6-0: 61823; 61855; 61857; 61876; 61878; 61879; 61881; 61885; 61897; 61900; 61909; 61911; 61916; 61924; 61928; 61931; 61933; 61955; 61968; 61983; 61988; 61990; 61991; 61992
D30/2 4-4-0: 62421 LAIRD O'MONKBARNS; 62424 CLAVERHOUSE; 62435 NORNA
D34 4-4-0: 62471 GLEN FALLOCH; 62483 GLEN GARRY; 62484 GLEN LYON; 62487 GLEN ARKLET; 62488 GLEN ALADALE; 62490 GLEN FINTAIG; 62494 GLEN GOUR
D49/1 4-4-0: 62702 OXFORDSHIRE; 62711 DUMBARTONSHIRE; 62712 MORAYSHIRE; 62715 ROXBURGHSHIRE; 62721 WARWICKSHIRE
J35 0-6-0: 64462; 64479; 64486; 64489; 64492; 64506; 64512; 64515; 64517; 64518; 64519; 64523; 64524; 64527; 64532; 64533; 64535
J37 0-6-0: 64538; 64543; 64547; 64552; 64555; 64557; 64562; 64566; 64572; 64576; 64577; 64582; 64586; 64594; 64595; 64599; 64603; 64605; 64606; 64607; 64608; 64614; 64624; 64625; 64636; 64637
J39 0-6-0: 64794; 64946; 64963; 64986
J36 0-6-0: 65224 MONS; 65251; 65258; 65267; 65286; 65288; 65292; 65305; 65310; 65311; 65316; 65334
J24 0-6-0: 65617; 65623
J38 0-6-0: 65906; 65912; 65914; 65915; 65918; 65919; 65920; 65927; 65929
C16 4-4-2T: 67492; 67494; 67495; 67496; 67497
V1/V3 2-6-2T: 67605; 67606; 67607; 67608; 67609; 67617; 67624; 67629; 67630; 67649; 67659; 67666; 67670
Y9 0-4-0ST: 68092; 68093; 68095; 68096; 68097; 68098; 68099; 68102; 68105; 68111; 68115; 68119; 68122
J88 0-6-0T: 68320; 68325; 68334; 68338; 68340; 68342; 68348; 68352
J83 0-6-0T: 68448; 68449; 68450; 68454; 68463; 68464; 68469; 68472; 68474; 68477
J67/J69 0-6-0T: 68492; 68505; 68511; 68525; 68562; 68623
J50 0-6-0T: 68952
N15 0-6-2T: 69130; 69133; 69134; 69140; 69141; 69144; 69146; 69147; 69148; 69149; 69152; 69167; 69168; 69172; 69173; 69175; 69186; 69219
WD 2-8-0: 90038; 90114; 90248; 90289; 90291; 90376; 90436; 90468; 90469; 90493; 90496; 90555

Holmes 0-6-0s (LNER J36) had been employed on mineral and goods traffic around Edinburgh since the 1880s, but early in the new century the North British decided that a more powerful six-coupled engine was needed for long distance workings. The result was Reid's class B 0-6-0s (LNER J35), 76 of which were built between 1906 and 1913. St Margarets was one of the first sheds to receive them and had around seventeen on its books for several decades. They appeared on passenger trains to Glasgow between the wars and were also sprightly enough to work morning business trains from North Berwick. J35 64489 stands alongside the coaling stage at St Margarets on 23 May 1953. Built by North British Loco Co, it entered service as 202 in September 1909, became LNER 9202 and was withdrawn in June 1961. Photograph John Robertson, The Transport Treasury.

On 18 August 1951, C16 67492 waits to be coaled at St Margarets after its work for the day had been completed. As Reid class L, the 21 4-4-2Ts which were built in 1915-21 proved to be the ultimate North British passenger tank design and the first to be superheated. 448, which became LNER 9448 and eventually BR 67492, was one of six such engines sent new to St Margarets from North British Loco Co, in this case during April 1916. At first they worked to Galashiels via Peebles and were a familiar sight on the 'Lothian Coast Express' from North Berwick. They tended to be marginalised by V1s and duties on the Polton, Penicuick, Musselburgh, Corstorphine and Suburban lines were well within their capacity. 67492 was withdrawn in March 1960. Photograph John Robertson, The Transport Treasury.

A delightful evening scene at St Margarets, probably during the autumn of 1948, showing a tiny fraction of the army of shunters allocated to the shed. Besides the two J83s, there is a J88 on the right and a Y9 on the far side of the turntable. 68449, the J83 in the foreground, was built by Neilson Reid in September 1900, became LNER 9802 and received its BR number during August 1948. In 1952 it was fitted with vacuum brakes for marshalling braked goods trains in South Leith yard and lasted until September 1958. The Y9 appears to be 8108, one of the Leith Dock 'pugs'. It was withdrawn as 68108 in November 1959 after nearly seventy years service. Residents of the tenements clearly needed to be tolerant of locomotive smoke! Photograph W Hermiston, The Transport Treasury.

A moment of torpor at St Margarets as grimy tanks languish in early evening sunshine around the turntable. It should be pointed out that several shunters at the shed, notably Y9s with regular crews, were kept in spotless external condition. Presumably 8325 is not in steam, otherwise the firebox would not be a suitable perch for a break and a game of cards! Although undated, the photograph must have been taken in the first half of 1946. J88 8325 had been 9841 until January of that year, whilst J83 9816 was renumbered 8463 in June 1946. The J88 was one of 35 short-wheelbase dock shunters with side tanks and outside cylinders, built between 1904 and 1914. Despite its scruffy condition here, the J83 became one of five painted in fully-lined BR black for pilot duties at Waverley. Although the 0-6-0Ts are more or less contemporary Reid designs, detail differences are of interest. The J88 has dumb buffers, no wing plates and cylinder lubricating tallow cups on the footplate. The J83 has vacuum brakes, wing plates and tallow cups on the smokebox. 68325 originated at Cowlairs in January 1905 and was condemned in March 1961. 68463 was built by Sharp Stewart in April 1901 and was withdrawn in November 1958. Photograph G. Whitelaw Collection.

A glance back from a train arriving in Edinburgh from the east around 1958 afforded this glimpse of N15 69141, one of the St Margarets 'unsung heroes' out on the road. The smart J83 passenger pilots were very much in the public eye, but the goods pilots tended to be unkempt and usually ventured only as far as Waverley depot. Although the N15s were probably best known as bankers on Cowlairs Incline out of Glasgow Queen Street, a total of 99 of these versatile, hard working engines were built between 1910 and 1924 and St Margarets had up to seventeen of them for various goods duties. 69141 was built by North British Loco Co as 397 in August 1910 and was withdrawn in September 1960. Photograph The Transport Treasury.

Diesel Dawn

Like most major stations, Waverley experienced a gradual transition from steam to new forms of traction. In this case it was creeping dieselisation, followed eventually by electrification of the East Coast main line from Kings Cross, the former Caledonian route to Carstairs for through workings to Glasgow Central, and the North Berwick branch involving the remaining local services from the east end bays. For devotees of steam, there was an ominous development in January 1957 when Swindon Inter-City diesel multiple units began working the intense service between Edinburgh and Glasgow Queen Street. The fastest trains managed this journey in 55 minutes, merely three minutes improvement on the schedules operated by Pacifics in 1938. However, it has to be admitted that most passengers considered the new diesels a substantial improvement on what went before. The pace of change accelerated early in 1958 when Gloucester diesel railcars started to operate an hourly service between North Berwick and Corstorphine via Waverley. Galashiels via Peebles and certain South Suburban workings were also turned over to these multiple units. English Electric Type 4s appeared on some East Coast expresses during the same year, but they were prone to failure and the A4s had a wonderful swansong on this route, proving that they were the true top dogs.

This brilliant spell for steam could not last and the introduction of English Electric Deltics on top jobs between Edinburgh and London in 1961 proved decisive. At the same time, Birmingham RCW/Sulzer Type 2s were becoming familiar on the Waverley route. From May 1971, BRCW diesels top and tailing Mk2 coaches between Waverley and Glasgow Queen Street cut the journey to 43 minutes. Another minute was shaved off when Brush Type 4s with Mk3 coaches were introduced in December 1980. Meanwhile, InterCity 125s, in popular parlance HSTs, had

Allocations at Haymarket (64B) 1966
English Electric Type 4: D260, D261, D262, D263, D264, D265, D266, D357, D358, D359, D360, D361, D362, D363, D364, D365, D366, D367, D368
Brush Type 4: D1968, D1969, D1970, D1971, D1972, D1973, D1974, D1975, D1976
North British 0-4-0 Shunter: D2751, D2752, D2753
BR 0-6-0 Shunter: D3554, D3555, D3560, D3738, D3739, D3742, D3877, D3879
Derby-Sulzer Type 2: D5061, D5062, D5064, D5065, D5066, D5068, D5069, D5070, D5071, D5072, D5094, D5095
Birmingham RC&W Type 2: D5300, D5301, D5302, D5303, D5304, D5305, D5306, D5307, D5308, D5309, D5310, D5311, D5312, D5313, D5314, D5315, D5316, D5317, D5318, D5319
English Electric Type 3: D6837, D6838, D6844, D6845, D6846, D6847, D6848, D6849, D6850, D6851, D6858
English Electric Type 1: D8028, D8029, D8030
Clayton Type 1 (Mostly based at Millerhill depot): D8554, D8555, D8556, D8557, D8558, D8559, D8560, D8561, D8562, D8563, D8564, D8565, D8566, D8567, D8568, D8569, D8570, D8571, D8572, D8573, D8574, D8575, D8576, D8577, D8578, D8579, D8580, D8581, D8582, D8583, D8584, D8585, D8586, D8587, D8604, D8605, D8606, D8607, D8608, D8609, D8610, D8611, D8612, D8613, D8614, D8615, D8616
English Electric 'Deltic' Type 5: D9000 ROYAL SCOTS GREY, D9004 QUEEN'S OWN HIGHLANDER, D9006 THE FIFE AND FORFAR YEOMANRY, D9010 THE KING'S OWN SCOTTISH BORDERER, D9013 THE BLACK WATCH, D9016 GORDON HIGHLANDER, D9019 ROYAL HIGHLAND FUSILIER, D9021 ARGYLL AND SUTHERLAND HIGHLANDER

Allocations at St Margarets (64A) 1966
4MT 2-6-4T: 42128
5MT 4-6-0: 45053, 45162, 45168, 45469, 45483
V2 2-6-2: 60824, 60868, 60955, 60976
B1 4-6-0: 61307
J36 0-6-0: 65234, 65319
2MT 2-6-0: 78046
4MT 2-6-4T: 80114, 80124
North British 0-4-0 Shunter: D2705, D2706, D2710, D2712, D2714, D2715, D2721, D2723, D2724, D2725, D2727, D2728, D2729, D2744, D2745, D2746, D2747, D2748, D2749, D2750, D2754, D2755
BR 0-6-0 Shunter: D3547, D3548, D3561, D3728, D3729, D3730, D3731, D3732, D3733, D3878, D3880, D3881, D3882, D3883, D3884, D3885, D3886, D3887, D3888, D3889, D3890, D3891, D3892

Just after diesel dawn, this scene is Princes Street Gardens on 15 August 1959. The 4.00pm for Glasgow Queen Street, formed by a fairly new Swindon Inter-City set, emerges from Mound Tunnel as A2 60530 SAYAJIRAO on the 4.00pm departure for Perth steals the lead and leaves a trail of exhaust in the path of the upstart dmu. A few people among the Edinburgh Festival crowds in front of the National Gallery are distracted by activity on the railway, but the classic 4.00pm departures have lost a little of their shine during the transition from steam to diesel. 60530 has a residual red and cream coach in its consist, while the Swindon set displays the code 'A', denoting an express. Photograph John Robertson, The Transport Treasury.

taken over certain Deltic turns in 1978. Electrification brought Class 91s and Mk4 coaches to the East Coast main line in 1991. Today, Waverley is attuned to the privatised system, with GNER's dark blue trains following the route of the Pacifics to London, Virgin's red and silver Voyagers on cross-country services and Scotrail's multi-coloured Turbos providing frequent departures for Glasgow. A lot has changed at Wonderful Waverley since steam was in its heyday, but the Castle, Scott Monument, Hotel and Governor's House remain the same. They have seen it all!

Below. Even this tribute to the glorious days of steam at Waverley cannot ignore the Deltics, the most charismatic diesels ever and a class embraced by Haymarket drivers of the 1960s and 1970s almost as much as their predecessors revered Pacifics in the 1940s and 1950s. Technology had moved on of course, and Edinburgh's big English Electrics invariably went all the way to Kings Cross in normal service. Although this echoed non-stop steam workings on the 'Flying Scotsman' and 'Elizabethan', most Haymarket Pacifics rarely ventured south of Newcastle. In this mid-1960s view, an unidentified Deltic in two-tone green has arrived at Waverley with the down 'Flying Scotsman'. The wonderful headboard does not need a name to identify the train. Photograph The Transport Treasury.

Bottom. On 15 November 1964, A4 60019 BITTERN, with a special from Aberdeen threads Princes Street Gardens as a Derby-Sulzer 'Peak' emerges from Mound Tunnel on a service train from Newcastle to Glasgow Queen Street. BITTERN was new to Heaton as 4464 in December 1937, but moved to Gateshead in March 1943 and remained there for twenty years. When the fast afternoon service from Edinburgh to Kings Cross known as 'The Talisman' was introduced on 17 September 1956, 60019 took the first up train from Newcastle to Kings Cross. In October 1963, BITTERN was temporarily based at St Margarets before going to Aberdeen the next month to work the three hour expresses to Glasgow Buchanan Street, which it did for almost three years. Preservation followed withdrawal in September 1966. Photograph The Transport Treasury.

With the end of steam only a few years away, several specials were organised in the early 1960s to commemorate the end of a magnificent era. At Waverley on 2 June 1962, that most famous of A4s, 60022 MALLARD, draws forward from the 'Aberdeen Flyer'. The special, organised by the RCTS, was supposed to be the last non-stop steam run between Kings Cross and Edinburgh, but it was marred by a signal check at Chathill. Haymarket replaced 60022 with 60004 WILLIAM WHITELAW for the onward leg to Aberdeen and MALLARD returned south on 5 June with a Motorail car-carrier to Holloway. The very last timetabled non-stop run between London and Edinburgh was made by 60022 on 8 September 1961, the up train being hauled by 60009 UNION OF SOUTH AFRICA of Haymarket. MALLARD was never based in Scotland, going to Doncaster as 4468 in March 1938, Grantham in October 1943 and Kings Cross in April 1948. It was withdrawn in April 1963 and subsequently preserved, almost inevitable in view of its 125mph sprint on 3 July 1938. Photograph The Transport Treasury.

It is almost goodbye to steam at Waverley. On a grey morning in 1965, V2 60919 waits with a train for Dundee, flanked by Haymarket diesel shunter D3738 on station pilot duties and a Swindon Inter-City dmu on a Glasgow Queen Street service. This was not a good time for the railway in Edinburgh, as signs of neglect and accumulated grime are everywhere. Much has changed since then. Waverley is now very smart, although cluttered with the electrification equipment essential for a modern railway. The pilots have gone and after a period of push-pull diesel operation, followed by 158s, Glasgow services are now provided by Scotrail class 170 Turbostars. The North British Hotel has been spruced up and is now The Balmoral. By early 2003, redevelopment of the station was proposed, though hopefully the essential character will be kept. In many ways, Waverley still is wonderful! Photograph J.A.M. Vaughan, The Transport Treasury.

Truly Magnificent

A last look at the might of steam in Edinburgh and what better than one of Gresley's P2 2-8-2s. Thompson may have detested them and they certainly had their faults, but they were a bold attempt to solve the problem of increasing loads on the difficult route to Aberdeen. They were also very much natives of Edinburgh. A final glimpse of the National Gallery of Scotland and Princes Street Gardens as 2001 COCK O' THE NORTH heads towards the Forth Bridge with the 5.15pm express for Aberdeen, probably in the summer of 1936 or 1937. This train conveyed through coaches from the down 'Flying Scotsman' which had arrived at platform 11. As a result, it is crossing from the down Glasgow to down Fife line. Photograph The Transport Treasury.